Charles B. Galloway

Modern missions: their evidential value

(Cole lectures for 1896)

Charles B. Galloway

Modern missions: their evidential value
(Cole lectures for 1896)

ISBN/EAN: 9783743334540

Manufactured in Europe, USA, Canada, Australia, Japa

Cover: Foto ©Lupo / pixelio.de

Manufactured and distributed by brebook publishing software (www.brebook.com)

Charles B. Galloway

Modern missions: their evidential value

MODERN MISSIONS:

THEIR EVIDENTIAL VALUE.

(COLE LECTURES FOR 1896.)

BY CHARLES B. GALLOWAY, D.D., LL.D.,
A Bishop of the Methodist Episcopal Church, South.

NASHVILLE, TENN.:
PUBLISHING HOUSE METHODIST EPISCOPAL CHURCH, SOUTH.
BARBEE & SMITH, AGENTS.
1896.

Entered, according to Act of Congress, in the year 1896,
BY THE BOARD OF TRUST OF VANDERBILT UNIVERSITY,
In the Office of the Librarian of Congress, at Washington.

CONTENTS.

LECTURE I.
THE QUESTION STATED; OR, THE ANSWERING VOICE OF HISTORY 1

LECTURE II.
CHRISTIANITY AND OTHER RELIGIONS 35

LECTURE III.
PORTABLE EVIDENCES FROM MANY LANDS.... 77

LECTURE IV.
FRUITS FROM VARIOUS FIELDS............... 115

LECTURE V.
THE MESSAGE OF MISSIONS TO THE CHURCH .. 155

LECTURE VI.
LESSONS FROM SOME MASTER MISSIONARIES .. 193

THE QUESTIONHE AN-
SWERINGY.

I.

THE QUESTION STATED; OR, THE ANSWERING VOICE OF HISTORY.

THE subject selected for this course of lectures by the Faculty extending the invitation is my apology for accepting a service for which, by taste and training, I have an unaffected sense of unfitness. The subject, and not the position, though most honorable, constrained my acceptance and accounts for my appearance. Having recently enjoyed the privilege of inspecting several of the great mission fields of the world, it seemed incongruous that I should positively decline, however meager might be my contribution to the discussion of so exalted a theme. The subject contemplates not so much a plea for Missions as a study of Missions, not so much an enforcement of obligation as a report of the results of investigation. It is hoped, however, that the report and its study will prove a persuasive plea for Missions and an additional enforcement of our divine indebtedness to the Christless world. Such a line of argument, harmonizing as it does with the energetic and practical life of the age, ought to be the strongest and most impregnable defense of our Christian religion. There is no enthusiasm in apologetics which are no more than "a vindication of the original guarantees of Christianity or of the documents in which it was first enshrined." That line of apology is not to be underrated, nor is it to be overestimated. A religion that is "merely capable of defense" can never command the homage of mankind, and will never stir the "enthusiasm of humanity." Canon Freemantle has thus forcefully characterized the essential quality of religion: "It must inspire and lead, or else it dies. We must show that it is capable of influencing, stimulating, and guiding the progress of humanity; and, further, that the world itself demands the Christian religion as alone capable of sustaining its hope and its energy."

My appointment, therefore, is to speak more as a witness than an advocate—to testify rather than to defend. I shall not consider the grounds and obligations of Missions—will not attempt to set forth the principles underlying, or the motives inspiring, or the authority requiring, a world-wide evangelism—but will turn an ear to the fields themselves and listen to the message they have to send. We are to "ask the days that are past" and passing, and give earnest heed to the "answering voice of history." We will consider not so much what the Scriptures command as what experience confirms. Thus we will ascertain some of the great truths modern Missions disclose and exemplify. If, as has been declared, "history is the supreme test of all things," we are concerned to know its verdict as to the virtue and power of the gospel to redeem the nations.

Dr. Fairbairn has said that "it is the function of the philosophic historian, the man of science in the field of religion, to get by analysis at the whole history of the genesis of the ideas that create our religious institutions." So ambitious a purpose is not contemplated in these lectures; but the facilities and materials for such a searching and final analysis are at hand, and have been furnished by the missionaries. We occupy the highest vantage point in history for the thorough study of Christianity. By virtue of this fact, we are better able than any former generation to form a correct estimate of its spirit, doctrines, and ethical system, *as compared with other religions*. And for this, by general admission, we are indebted to the achievements and revelations of modern Missions. They have not only illustrated the power of Christianity as a redemptive agency, but have also introduced the world to a larger acquaintance with all religions. We have broader knowledge of the life and literature of hitherto unknown peoples, and are in consequent possession of "a key to hearts and intellects which previously were closed to our approach." If, therefore, our plan of argument does not require an attempt to ascertain the "genesis" of religious ideas, we will try to trace their influence—will go down the stream, especially of modern history, and see if it be true in fact, as Ezekiel saw in vision, that "everything shall live whither the river cometh."

Bernard, in his Bampton Lectures on "The Progress of Doctrine in the New Testament," observes that "every age, every Church, every sect, every controversy, in some way or other contributes something to the working out, the testing, or the illustrating of some part of the revelation of God." Our inquiry, therefore, will be as to what disclosures modern Missions have made to the Church—what additions to the history of Christian doctrine and what distinct contributions to the evidence and defense of the gospel. It is asserted that Christianity is inherently expansive and progressive—that its nature is to grow. The growing years should, therefore, be a continuing display of its divine character—a revelation of Christ additional to the thrilling records of the

New Testament, and a constant "evolution of the Holy Ghost" in the rational and moral consciousness of the Church. And this is the Christian's high claim. He contends not with Dionysius that "history is philosophy teaching by examples," nor with Matthew Arnold that it is a mere "stream of tendency," but rather that history is the movement of God in providence and grace. That as in the Old Testament history there is an unmistakable discernment of "one Presence and one increasing purpose," so the later history of the Church, especially the story of missionary endeavor, reveals a Saviour "come and coming," and one "mighty to save."

The divine purpose to make the progress of the Church a "continuous and cumulative exhibition" of Christ as the world's Redeemer and Lord is thus stated by Bishop Westcott in a single luminous sentence: "The history of Christianity is the *history of the slow and progressive efforts* that have been made to gain and to embody an adequate knowledge of Christ in the fullness of his twofold nature, of the eternal revealed under the conditions of time, of the earthly raised to the heavenly, of the harmony that is established potentially between man and humanity and God, under the continuous guiding of the living Spirit."

Now it is the aim of these lectures to discover, if possible, how far this divine ideal has been made actual in the history of modern Missions. This should not be a very difficult task, for Christianity is essentially historical. It is " not a mere spirit, a spirit unclothed;" but projects itself into the life and institutions of the world, and seeks to mold and control them for its own lofty and beneficent ends. It is, therefore, a religion of facts as well as ideas, and by those facts its ideas are to be tested and its virtues measured. And if they stand the test, which ought to be searching and severe, the argument is complete; for as Dr. Fairbairn has well said, "There is no logic like the logic of fact; there is no law of reason so inevitable as the law that fulfills itself in historical movement."

And this is God's favorite method of instruction and revelation. The Scriptures are largely given up to *narrative*. The Bible is not so much a manual of doctrine as the story of God's dealings with man and men. It is a "book of models as well as maxims," and Christ's ministry was a ministry of works rather than of words. Though "he spake as never man spake," he wrought more than he talked. Indeed, his method was first to act a truth, and then proclaim it; to do it, and then *declare* it. And this accords perfectly with man's mental and spiritual capacity; for truth is best apprehended, not by studying precepts and proverbs, but by observing its influence upon human life and conduct. The moral law itself is best understood, not by reading its "shalts" and "shalt nots," but by "witnessing the course of Providence in the actual career of good and evil men."

But while the task of ascertaining the philosophy of history seems not to be difficult, as a matter of fact it is by no means easy. Two persons may look at the same facts and learn therefrom very different, if not antagonistic, lessons. A distinguished writer has said: "History is no sphinx. She tells us what kind of teaching has been fruitful in blessing to humanity, and why, and what has been a mere boastful promise or powerless formula." That depends largely, though not entirely, upon who consults the oracles, and *for* what he is listening. Edward Gibbon, for instance, of whom it has been said, " no man ever clothed a sneer in language so stately, or mocked in periods so majestic," in writing his great history evidently made a studied effort to avoid any recognition of Christianity, and only acknowledged its benign influences when compelled to do so by facts that even the blind could not fail to see. So, then, in order rightly to interpret the true philosophy of events, we must not only take into account the fact that "history has its *foreground* and its *background*," but our own personal and spiritual attitude thereto. As we are we see. Only a spiritual eye can discern spiritual verities. The one essential preparation for a correct understanding of religious history is thus stated in a few wise words by a great thinker: "Nothing but deep initiation into the spirit of the Bible can enable us to form the faintest idea as to what historical events belong most to the divine plan, or have most relation to the kingdom of the eternities."

Now these preliminary suggestions are offered, not as a plea in abatement or to escape the full force of the fiercest criticism, but as a guide in our further investigations. Christianity has asserted claims and made a history, and by that history must stand or fall. Of course it should only be held responsible for its legitimate fruits. Its Founder bore the sins of the world, but should not be charged with all the failures and follies of the world. But Christianity has set up claims which are audacious if not true, and encouraged hopes that are cruel and criminal if beyond possible realization. If Christianity is only an *ad interim* stage in human development, without elements of permanency or promise of universality;

if it is only one of many religions; if it is simply suited to the genius of a particular people, especially the Western mind at a certain stage of civilization; if it is not necessary to every child of Adam—then its claims are the sublimest arrogance and its history an unparalleled travesty. And, as Canon Liddon has aptly phrased it, the "missionary enterprise is at once wasteful and impertinent." It is recklessly wasteful of home resources and an impertinent interference with other beneficent religions and civilizations. If it is not the answer, and the *only* "answer to every religious aspiration and need of man and men," if it is not the *only* "power of God unto salvation," then St. Paul's sense of indebtedness to Greek and barbarian was a burdensome delusion, and his wearisome missionary labors were nothing less than prodigious folly.

The claims of Christianity are absolute and universal. Its certain conquest of the world is affirmed as positively as the very existence of God, on whom it is conditioned. "As truly as I live, all the earth shall be filled with the glory of the Lord." And Daniel declared that "his dominion is an everlasting dominion, and his kingdom that which shall not be destroyed." St. Paul affirmed "that in the dispensation of the fullness of times he might gather together in one all things in Christ, both which are in heaven, and which are on earth." The apostle sublimely contemplated a vast, united kingdom, consisting of the unfallen in heaven and the restored on earth, all under the common lordship of Jesus Christ. Now, in enunciating the principles of that "kingdom of God," and in enforcing the divine obligation to hasten its coming, two dreadful alternatives are distinctly declared: (1) The Church will be condemned for neglect of the heathen; (2) the heathen will be doomed to perpetual degradation because of that neglect. Every honest student of religion has a right, therefore, to ask: "What are the results of the efforts already made? At the close of this last and most active century of vast expenditure of time, treasure, and human life, what are the returns? And what do the facts attest?" If true to the principles announced and claimed to be of divine authority, if in any sense they are a fulfillment of promises made, promises said to be of God and characterized as "exceeding great and precious," Missions ought to be the "actual and historical expression of the precepts of the gospel." The facts must indicate the factors. I accept the statement that "the word of God and the work of God must agree, and we must know the former in order to

THE QUESTION STATED. 13

interpret the latter;" but this also we have a right to demand—that the latter must be a clear expression and faithful fulfillment of the former.

The appeal for continued and increased support of an enterprise must be reënforced by its hope of advancement. A failing cause cannot command enthusiastic support; a trailing flag never stirs the heart of hope. I do not mean that mere numbers measure progress, that statistics alone gauge success, that truth depends upon majorities. Max Müller made a reply to Canon Taylor (who was at once frightened by his own figures and strangely enamored with Islamism) that was as apt as it was philosophical: "If I gain ten, I am right; if somebody else gains twelve, then I am wrong." Thus he exposed the absurdity of the mere mathematics of religion.

But there is inspiration in success. Once the Church depended solely for encouragement on the positive command of God to "Go," and the promise of the Holy Spirit's constant presence and guidance. Now, in addition, we have an unabridged volume of testimony to the gospel's redeeming power in the history of Missions, every glorious page of which gleams with light and thrills with fervor and spiritual energy.

It will be the purpose of these lectures, therefore, in a survey of this century of modern Missions, to consider:

1. What changes have been wrought?
2. Have the changes been beneficent?
3. Are they so directly traceable to Christian and missionary influences as to justify the challenge to the world to see "What hath God wrought?"
4. What emphasis is given to Christian evidences thereby, and what new lessons in Christian life and doctrine do they teach?

Great changes have certainly been wrought. Mighty forces of some sort have been at work. The map of the world has shifted its shadings and colorings every few years during the past most eventful century. Society in some countries has been revolutionized from top to bottom. The principles of government have been radically modified. Autocracies have given way to constitutions, monarchs have bowed to parliaments, and barbarous tribes have accepted the protectorate of Christian nations; and even in Christian countries, as the author of "Ecce Homo!" observes, "the present century has witnessed a remarkable softening of manners." Legal tortures for convicted crime have been abolished, civil severities have been swept away, and in private life "men have greatly advanced in tenderness, sympathy, and unwillingness to inflict pain."

Isolation has yielded to a world-wide spirit of neighborhood, and the most frigid exclusiveness has been compelled to surrender to the warmth of an international hospitality. Long-locked ports have been opened, and are now eagerly bidding for the commerce of the world. Except in a few countries, notably in Turkey, there is tolerance of religious opinion. Though persecution has not entirely ceased, there is less and less danger to life and liberty in professing and propagating any form of religion. Japan, an empire of forty millions of people, once the most exclusive of hermit nations, and which less than fifty years ago prohibited the introduction of Christianity on penalty of death, is now as tolerant in opinion and as open to the gospel as the most Christian nation. And her broad, progressive purpose for the future, by imperial edict, was announced several years ago in these words: "It is intended that henceforth education shall be so diffused that there may not be a village with an ignorant family, nor a family with an ignorant member." Railways have made a network of the whole empire, telegraph lines stretch from one end of the land to the other, daily newspapers abound, banks and hospitals have been established, and they have a mail service equal to the post office department of the United States. Corea, though the last to emerge from her hermitage, has given the hand of welcome to other nations, and opened her doors to the ambassadors of Christ. Siam gives ample governmental protection, and even royal welcome, to missionaries. Africa, until a few years ago the great unknown and unexplored, to-day is the rallying ground of all the great Christian nations eagerly prosecuting their political, commercial, and missionary enterprises. China has seen her great wall broken, and the breach can never be healed. A recent imperial edict declared that "the several nations are at liberty to promulgate their religions in China as set forth in the treaties, and imperial decrees have been granted instructing the various provinces to give protection at all times. The religion of the Western countries simply admonishes people to become virtuous, and the native converts are Christian subjects under the jurisdiction of local officials. *The religions and peoples ought to exist peaceably side by side.*" And equally as momentous is the news just received, that among the matriculates in the Methodist University at Peking for the present term are a grandson of the private tutor of the last emperor of China, a nephew of the private tutor of the present emperor, a son of the imperial commissioner of Chinese railways, and fourteen of the proud *literati* of the kingdom.

India has passed entirely under Christian influence, with over two millions of Christian adherents, and more communicants than the apostles and early disciples gathered in the whole world during the first century of the Christian era.

Many of the cannibal islands of the South Seas have ceased to celebrate their horrid feasts, have burned their idols, and are now reverently bowing to the scepter of the Son of God. In Fiji, where a hundred years ago there was not a single Christian, there is to-day not a single heathen, and in a population of one hundred and twenty thousand not a single home in which there is not morning and evening worship. And countries like Mexico and Brazil, for centuries dominated by a corrupt form of Christianity, scarcely elevated in its ethical results above the false faiths of the East, have been thrown wide open to a purer and larger life.

And there has also been a momentous *change in the Church's attitude* to, and estimate of, the cause of Missions. We are a full millennium from the age and sneer of Sydney Smith, though the almanac records only one hundred years. No Christian minister would now be tolerated with such a narrow and intolerant spirit—one who would dare ridicule a cause "in which the Spirit of God mingles, and which the providence of God molds." He anathematized William Carey and his associates as "didactic artisans, whose proper talk is of bullocks and not of the gospel; delirious mechanics; the lowest of the people; detachments of lunatics." And that Christian assembly would be an anachronism whose presiding officer would say to some modern William Carey: "Young man, sit down! When God pleases to convert the heathen, he will convert them without your aid or mine." No Scottish General Assembly could now be gathered that would pronounce the missionary idea "highly preposterous," or have the temerity to praise "the happy ignorance of the untutored savage." No bishop of the Church of England would now so minimize the mission of the gospel or discount the apostolic history of the Church Missionary Society as to publicly and privately argue against the idea of the missionary enterprise. The days of such ignorance the Church would not now wink at.

Every Church is awake and at work. Organizations have multiplied until about five hundred and sixty-one societies are actively engaged in advancing the enterprise of Foreign Missions. The offerings to this sacred cause have increased from the £13 2s. 6d. of the humble Kettering Baptists to a yearly contribution of $15,000,000. There are three societies in America that expend annually over $1,000,000 each in sending the gospel to the regions beyond. Medical missions are carrying healing in their hands, and thereby opening highways into the hearts of nations and millions for the triumphal incoming of the Son of God. And simultaneous with this work came the new apostolate of woman. To her heathen sisters she is carrying the tender words of the Christ, who alone in all this world has made woman conscious of her womanhood. Seventy-two societies have already been organized, and their lines have gone out into all the earth.

And what a change in the world's attitude toward missionaries! The men once derided as "detachments of lunatics," are now uppermost in public esteem. David Livingstone, once ridiculed as a fanatic, was given a State funeral and sepulture in Westminster Abbey. The East India Company formally expressed its estimate of Christian Missions in these rather sarcastic words: "The sending of Christian missionaries into our Eastern possessions is the maddest, most expensive, most unwarranted project that was ever proposed by a lunatic enthusiast." It violently opposed the coming of William Carey and his colaborers, and they were compelled to seek shelter under a Danish flag. But what a change was wrought! When Carey had finished his course—had accomplished his marvelous work and peacefully fallen asleep—that same East India Company lowered its flags to half-mast on the day of his funeral, and honored the "consecrated cobbler" as though he had been a viceroy or a general of armies.

Dean Farrar, in referring to the sneer of Sydney Smith against William Carey and the small contribution of £13 2s. 6d. by the Baptists of Kettering to project a mission in India, uttered these generous and eloquent words: "Nevertheless, at this moment every one who knows anything of India knows that we owe more to that consecrated cobbler, and to his pitiful and beggarly £13 2s. 6d., than we owe to the genius of Warren Hastings, or the fiery battle brunt of Lord Clive."

And the *London Times*, once scornfully antagonistic and abusive, now comes to the defense of missionaries, vigorously rebukes those who scoff at their reports as the visions of harmless enthusiasts, and pays this tribute to Drs. Moffatt and Livingstone:

Moffatt, it may be said, has labored, and other men have entered into his labor. Livingstone has come after him, and has gone beyond him and has linked his memory forever with the records of the South African Church. The progress of South Africa has been mainly due to men of Moffatt's stamp. In him, as in David Livingstone, it is hard to say which character has predominated, that of the missionary proper or that of the teacher and guide. Certain it is that, apart from the special stimulus they felt as proclaimers of the gospel message, they would never have thrown themselves as they did into the work in which their lives were consecrated. It was by no zeal for the spread of civilization on its own account that they passed many years laboring and teaching among savage tribes, amid dangers of every kind, amid privations of which they themselves made light, but which only a sense of their high spiritual mission could have prompted them to face and undergo.

And I quote again from that great organ of public opinion in its tribute to missionaries in China, and its high estimate of their mighty labors. It says:

The only real interpreter of thought and progress of the West to the millions of China is the missionary; and when we remember that European knowledge of China is derived almost wholly from the works of missionaries, we may fairly say that these men stand as interpreters between the East and the West As to the charity, we can only answer that China had no efficient hospitals or medical attendance until the missionaries established them, and in truth she has no other now; and when her great men, such as Li Hung Chang and Prince Chun, are in serious danger they have to go to the despised missionary doctor for that efficient aid which no Chinaman can give them.

But even more remarkable is the following paragraph from the learned pages of a recent issue of the *London Quarterly Review:*

> Men of mark for scholarship, in larger numbers than ever, devote their talents to the labor or the literature of the mission field and add to its prestige. The sons of English bishops no longer monopolize the richest livings at home, but give themselves to this most trying form of Church work abroad; and the sees of Litchfield and Exeter and Hereford, and even the princely throne of Durham, are adding to their dignity by sending from episcopal palace and castle those who might justly expect high honor and advancement here in England. An archbishop's daughter maintained for years single-handed the work of educating Arab boys in Egypt, and daughters of lay peers superintend and cheer by their presence the zenana workers in India. Cambridge dispatched the most learned of its Arabic professors to try and win the Mohammedans of Aden, and the foremost of its cricketers to no less arduous work in China.

But while remarkable changes of sentiment at home and abroad have been wrought, and recognition, often reluctant, has been accorded, oppositon has not ceased. The point of attack has only been shifted.

The assertion is boldly made that Missions are a failure, and the reason given therefor is that Christianity is not adapted to Oriental peoples; that while it may suit the Western mind, it can never be permanently planted in the East; that it is as impossible as to try "to graft the tropic palm upon the Northern pine." To this defiant declaration the friends of Christianity reply that Missions have not only been a success, but they have been a triumph. They even go so far as, in the language of the Bishop of Ripon, to say that "the story of modern Missions is a continuation of the Acts of the Apostles, with all its essential supernaturalism;" that "prophecy links hands with Providence" to produce stupendous results in which the living Spirit has been found as well as promised. And to the assertion that Christianity is not suited to all people they reply that Christ is "the cotemporary of all ages," the omnipresent Factor of history, the omnipotent Force of the centuries, the guiding Spirit of the race; that Christianity is indigenous to every soil, and is *at home* everywhere; that its every domicile is a temple—a temple of the Holy Ghost—and the heart of its every true disciple is at once an altar and a throne.

Some tourists and residents of the merchant and official classes have failed to discover the results of evangelical effort as reported by the missionaries in such glowing terms. Not only so, but they have positively denied the truth of their statements, and pronounced their labors not only fruitless of good, but harmful and irritating. And some prominent natives also—the priestly champions of antagonistic and evidently decaying faiths—have been equally positive in pronouncing modern Missions a failure, and have analyzed the reasons therefor. A German tourist and author, Max Büchner, says that he always begins by dividing the assertions of missionaries by ten. And that same gentleman, to the no small amusement of those at all informed, also said: "Mission stations, since the last war in New Zealand, seem scarcely to exist any more as in former times." A naturalist, writing of the Ostiasks, expressed the wish "that they might long remain heathen, lest their good qualities should be lost." So able an organ of public opinion as the *Philadelphia Record* has been betrayed into so monstrous a declaration as this: "It has been estimated by well informed authorities that it takes an average of over two million dollars to convert one Chinaman; and the worst of it is that, for every Chinaman converted to Christianity, at least a thousand Christians have been converted into corpses."

Such statements should not be summarily set aside or impatiently resented because they disappoint our wishes and humiliate our ardent faith. If the Christian religion has demonstrated its inadequacy to meet the wants of any people; if it fails to sustain its high claims to be the light and life of every land it touches, to force it upon such countries and peoples is little less than a crime.

But these declarations, however positively made, do not necessarily impeach the testimony of missionaries. First of all, we must study the competency of witnesses. And several things are to be considered:

1. The personal attitude of the witness to the question. His supposed individual interest may prompt an adverse judgment. The doctrines preached, if they become dominant, might injure his immoral business. And for illustrations of that fact we have only to read the missionary history of Dr. John G. Paton, the apostle of the South Seas. Or he may be personally hostile because the missionary's presence and preaching are a rebuke to his manner of life. So his personal enmity may color his testimony. It has been aptly said that there is a peculiarity about eyes: they see only what the heart desires. Ordinary tourists and irreligious resident tradesmen and officials may, therefore, be incompetent witnesses. They do not, because they cannot, see a kingdom that cometh not with observation. And the presence of this Godless class constitutes one of the gravest and most

difficult problems of the mission fields. There is sad significance in the remark of an observant Hindoo: "If all Englishmen lived such lives as Donald McLeod, India would soon be a Christian country."

This amusing story, found in the "Recollections of an Indian Missionary," seems to throw light on the trustworthiness of certain witnesses. Some thirty-five years ago a regiment from Benares passed through Cawnpore. The officers of that garrison gave their comrades a dinner, to which ladies were also invited. In the course of it a lady asked a captain of the regiment what the missionaries were doing in Benares. The captain assured her that there were no missionaries there.

"But they have an Orphan House there," replied the lady.

"Pardon me; there exists no institution of that kind," said the captain.

"But I pay a subscription to it annually."

"I believe that; but I was three years in Benares, and must have seen the institution if it existed."

Then the gentleman who sat at the lady's right-hand said quietly to her, "Wait a little;" and then he asked the captain, "Did you use to go to church, sir?"

"Yes, we are commanded to attend."

"But who preached in Benares, for there is no government chaplain there?"

"True, we had no *padres;* but the service was conducted by clergymen who were much beloved by our men."

"Strange, captain; you attended services which were conducted by missionaries, and you know nothing of the existence of these gentlemen."

"W-h-a-t! Were they missionaries?"

"Now, another question, sir. 'Did you ever see the long building in the street which leads by Sigra to Marawaddi?'"

"Certainly. It happened once that a fox was lost there, and I rode into the *compound*. There was a heap of little black rascals who grinned at me. They knew where the fox was, but would not tell me."

"Then you were in the precincts of the Orphan House of which the lady beside you spoke."

"Indeed! I did not know what it was. I took it for an indigo factory, or something of that sort."

And yet such witnesses testify with perfect assurance against missionary work, not only in India, but in all the fields of the world.

2. We must consider the capacity of the witness to apprehend that about which he speaks. An

untutored savage could not be expected to give an intelligent opinion about the system of Copernicus in astronomy, or the Baconian method in philosophy, or the value of jetties in hydraulics.

In the realm of the spiritual this fact is fundamental. The natural man perceiveth not the things of the spirit. An open, sympathetic mind is necessary in order to apprehend certain truths. There must be not only breadth and strength of mental grasp, but oneness of spirit, likeness of soul, sympathy of heart. The attitude of the heart is as important as the posture of the mind.

We may be in immediate presence of great verities and not know it. There is pathos in the Lord's reply to Philip: "Have I been so long time with you, and dost thou not know me, Philip?" There is an undertone of disappointment and sadness in the words. Our sight is determined by our spiritual insight.

But that sublime truths are discredited or denied is not necessarily an argument against their existence. We are told that if our ear nerves were sufficiently delicate, the most rapturous music could be caught from the rising and falling of the sap in the trees of the forest. This is described in an oft-quoted passage from Mr. Huxley: "The wonderful silence of a tropical forest is often due only to the dullness of our hearing; and could our ears catch the murmurs of these tiny maelstroms as they whirl in the innumerable myriads of living cells which constitute each tree, we should be stunned as with the roar of a great city."

The Bampton Lectures for 1894, on "Personality, Human and Divine," discuss with conspicuous ability and satisfaction the proposition that moral affinity is needful for the knowledge of a person. Our own natures must be in sympathy with one if we would really know him. Affinity is the condition of self-revelation on the one hand and of right understanding on the other. "He must become Godlike," says Plotinus, "who desires to see God."

So the Godless cannot interpret the divine. The irreligious are incompetent to pass judgment upon things spiritual. They cannot apprehend that for which they have been apprehended.

Another class that criticise Missions and are almost desperately demanding to be heard are *native heathen, especially of the priestly order*. Some educated Indian gentlemen (notably Mr. Telang, Mr. Gandhi, and Mr. Vivikananda) have recently pronounced severe judgment against mission work, and attempted to account for its humiliating failure. But these gentlemen, though natives and lifelong residents, are not necessarily informed in such matters. Indeed, it is a remarkable fact that such persons are generally the most incompetent witnesses. They are hostile to the cause about which they testify, and of necessity get their information second-hand.

And these native residents and disciples of an antagonistic faith differ among themselves. Mr. Vivekananda, who attracted so much attention as the representative of Hindooism at the "Congress of Religions," ventures to say of woman in India that "from the Hindoo standpoint she receives all her rights." Alas for the "standpoint!" But in opposition to that statement I give the testimony of another highly educated and unusually broad-minded Brahman, the editor of the *Hindu*, a leading paper in Southern India. In the columns of that journal he says:

> We recently approved the statement of a Bombay paper, that the social eminence which the Parsees so deservedly enjoy at the present moment is due to these two causes: that their women are well educated, and they are bound by no restrictions of caste. These two advantages make themselves felt among our native Christian brethren, and it is probable that they will soon be the Parsees of Southern India. They will furnish the most distinguished public servants, barristers, merchants, and citizens among the various classes of the native community.

But more significant is the report of the Ramabai Association, conducted by that remarkable Christian woman, Pundita Ramabai, in behalf of the child widows of India. It seems incredible that there are twenty-three million widows in India, of whom ten thousand one hundred and sixty-five are under four years of age, and fifty-one thousand eight hundred and seventy-five are between the ages of five and nine. Referring to the statement that the life of a child widow was not so hard and piteous as had been represented—that their bodies were not so " emaciated and disfigured by cruel blows," that the number of suicides and lives of shame was exaggerated—the last report says: "Let him who believes such statements, though made by the Hindoos themselves, come to the Saharada Sadana, listen to the pitiful stories of some of its inmates, see the white mark of the hot iron on the head, the little white scars made by the sharp finger nails meeting in the tender flesh of the face—as I have heard and seen all this, and much more—and he will not only know the truth, but he will feel it a privilege to do something for these unfortunate children." Thus the native witnesses widely disagree.

And even Mr. Telang, while expressing a Brahman's contempt for missionary interference and impertinence, is candid enough to say that "the structure of Hindoo society and religion is such that there is no such help for the Pariah as a Christian missionary has brought to him." As the mission of Christianity is to lift up the lowly and give the gospel of hope to the poorest, this is an unconscious tribute to its divine genesis and genius.

And there is yet another class of critics, who are found in the Church at home. They are represented by Canon Taylor and others, who, from what they regard as the slow progress of Missions, prophesy its failure. This class may not be large, but never fail to be heard. Such pessimism may result from an enfeebled faith or from infirmity of temper. Macaulay said that in his day he saw nothing but progress, yet he heard only of decay. There are always crises in the Church to some people—their faith is in a chronic state of panic. To them every discouragement is a calamity, and every seeming failure an utter defeat. They carry two small banners: one a danger signal, the other a flag of truce. At the first assault of an enemy they are ready to flee the field or run up a white flag. At the first rumble of thunder they forsake the house and rush for a storm pit. This is the faith of circumstances, not of eternal verities. They trust an arm of flesh, not a God "mighty to save."

But from whatever source these criticisms and objections emanate, and inspired by whatever motive, it is the function of the Christian apologist to give them judicial and thorough examination. If our Christianity fails in any of its high claims, we are most concerned to know it, and cannot afford to conceal it. But if we discover that its aims and claims are vindicated by the facts of history, then Lord Macaulay uttered a sober truth when he said: "Whoever does anything to depreciate Christianity is guilty of high treason against the civilization of mankind."

LECTURE II.

CHRISTIANITY AND OTHER RELIGIONS.

II.

CHRISTIANITY AND OTHER RELIGIONS.

RELIGION is the regnant power in this world. It molds the civilization and determines the destiny of nations. No such power resides elsewhere. Not in philosophy, not in science, not in art, not in climate, not in material resources, not in organized society—not in anything else are such mighty forces enfolded and such tremendous potentialities enthroned. It marks the progress of the race. It dominates individual life and determines personal conduct and character. Religion is universal and ineradicable. It is necessary to man, and, therefore, indestructible. So Prof. Tyndall said truly: "No atheistic reasoning can dislodge religion from the heart of man. As an experience of the consciousness it is perfectly beyond the assaults of logic."

The aim of this lecture is to study Christianity in contrast with the distinguishing characteristics of other religions. To this we are invited, if not impelled, by the high claims of the religion of Christ on the one hand, and by the bold challenge of its enemies on the other. It is not, however, within the scope of this discussion to consider the origin and development of religious beliefs, but to study their characteristics, and, if possible, trace their tendency and history. Whether, therefore, ancient religion began, as Schlegel argues, with the worship of the Supreme Being and in some countries lapsed into polytheism, or, as others contend, it started with ghost dreams and grew into monotheism, we are not just now concerned. It is true that the deism of Moslem is the monotheism of the Jew; and it may be, as is claimed, that the religion of the Zend-Avesta was borrowed from Abraham, and from the same patriarchal source also came the traditions that constructed Brahmanism and Persian Magianism. But into the history of the *genesis* of religious ideas I shall not enter. Our more practical purpose is to look at the chief characteristics of these great religions, as they are and have been, and examine their essential qualities and potential influences, as exhibited in the civilizations and history of nations.

Christianity claims to be the only true and universal religion, adapted to all men and needed by all men. It is absolute and exclusive. It recognizes no competitors and tolerates no rivals. Its attitude to other religions is antagonistic and uncompromising. The avowed purpose and certain effect of its teachings, as God assured Jeremiah when he ordained him "a prophet unto the nations," are "to root out, and to pull down, and to destroy, and to throw down, to build, and to plant." Its mission is destructive and constructive. It first extirpates and exterminates; then plants and builds. Now to this high claim and aggressive purpose the friends of other faiths make defiant denial. They claim to have the truth. They indignantly deny the adaptability of Christianity to all races, and positively affirm that Missions are a failure. A recent writer has stated that "Christ is not suited to the Hindoos." They desire a Saviour not so meek and lowly. There is also a revived disposition to applaud the merits of Mohammedanism and overestimate its civilizing power. Canon Taylor and others have boldly asserted its peculiar adaptation to the Eastern mind, and the superiority of its claims. And yet others consider it a good preparation for the higher Christian faith. But on the other hand, so high an authority as Sir William Muir gives this positive judgment: "They labor under a miserable delusion who suppose that Mohammedanism paves the way for a purer faith. No system could have been devised with more consummate skill for shutting out from the light and truth the nations over which it has sway. The sword of Mohammed and the Koran are the most fatal enemies of civilization, liberty, and truth that the world has yet known."

The doctrines, spirit, ethical systems, products, and historic effects of these religions will be briefly considered, and contrasted with the teachings, genius, and achievements of Christianity. By this method we can more readily ascertain the virtues and defects of the one or the other, and discover in which are those permanent and divine elements that will command the homage of the human soul and guarantee its final and eternal triumph. I readily accept the statement of Dr. Fairbairn that " the function of great beliefs is not to find perfect men, but to make them; to take the poor material it gets, and out of it to build up nobler characters and nobler men." The ethical value of any religion is tested by the kind of character it produces. Christianity, therefore, like every system of truth, should be measured by its declared purposes and legitimate effects.

It has been objected, however, that we have no right to infer the *truth* of a doctrine from its *utility;* that some beliefs may have been morally useful that were not true. To that objection Bishop Westcott makes convincing answer by showing that those beliefs were effective because not wholly false, and then utters these striking words: "And the absolute uniqueness of Christianity lies in this, that its capacity for good is universal and *in itself without alloy.*"

First, let us contrast Christianity and other religions *in their conceptions of God.* All religions are typed and determined by their deities. A people can never be better or worse than the gods they worship. A distinguished writer on comparative religions makes this very just observation: "A bad god can never have a good religion. As is the deity, such must the faith that is built on him be. Find out the character of the deity, and you find out the character of the religion." And on another occasion the same writer said: "There is no surer measure of a people's progress than its successive conceptions of the being it worships." It shall be our purpose, then, to ascertain, if possible, and from authoritative sources, what are those "conceptions" which constitute the religions of nations, and which determine their destiny.

We will look at Hindooism, the ancient religion of India, and see what is its conception of a being to worship. We find that there is no recognition of a personal God. It is pantheistic and idolatrous. There are lords many and gods many. As many as three hundred and thirty million divinities have been counted. The imagination has grown weary in their multiplication. One of the native writers of India, an ardent Brahman, the editor of the *Hindu*, said recently that Hindooism had never degraded itself so far as to believe in a personal God. A great scholar, and by no means unfriendly critic, makes this statement concerning the chief Hindoo deity: "Brahm is a sort of divine neuter, a colorless, abstract, superpersonal (and therefore impersonal) being, without love or anger, without sympathy or pity." There is also a sort of crude trinity—Brahma, Vishnu, and Siva—Vishnu representing the preserver and Siva the destroyer. Passions that would be base in men are sinless in their gods. Kali, the wife of Siva, the Moloch of India and a favorite goddess, is best propitiated by human sacrifices; has thugs to commit murder in her name, and is represented as a horrid black figure with protruding tongue, dripping blood, and usually adorned with a girdle of dangling hands and a necklace of human skulls.

Buddhism, a reformed religion which sprang up as a protest against Brahmanism, is substantially atheistic. In its creed there is no god to worship. Prof. Max Müller says: "Difficult as it seems to us to conceive, Buddha admits of no real cause of this unreal world. He denies the existence, not only of a creator, but of any absolute being."

Zoroastrianism, said to be the best and purest of all pagan creeds, believes in one god, but has no conception of him as a spiritual being; and its votaries worship first of all fire, then the sun, moon, stars, water, wind, earth, rivers, trees, etc., believing them to be emblems of the deity. They hold that the eternal created two gods: Ormuzd, the god of light, and Ahriman, the god of darkness. These two deities are in constant conflict, but in the end the god of light will triumph.

Mohammedism is monotheistic, but has a distorted conception of God. It is thus stated by Sir William Muir: "The god of Islam, solitary, severe, stern, inducing man to obey by motives that debase, depraving woman, hating the infidel, is a fit deity for wild Arabs or fierce Turks, but no god for civilized and free man." The Moslem creed may be expressed in a single sentence: "There is one god, and Mohammed is his prophet."

In this classification I have not included Confucianism, for it is a philosophy rather than a religion. Now with these crude and revolting ideas of a Being unto whom the soul of man cries, we contrast the new and noble conception of God which Christianity has introduced into the world:

A Person who is one Lord, self-existent, eternal, omnipotent, omniscient, the Creator and Preserver of all things, the everlasting and universal Father, full of mercy, truth, and tender compassion. He is a God who exercises tender watch care over every creature of his hand; a Lord whose overruling providence makes all things work for good to them that obey him; a loving Father who protects and provides for his children, and hears them when they pray; a Saviour who provides a remedy for all sin; a Spirit to regenerate, guide, inspire, and sanctify all that believe on his name. What a world-wide difference of conception! What a transfiguration in contrast with the pitiful conditions and heartless mockeries of the heathen world! With Dr. Martineau we all joyfully say: "A faith that spreads around and within the mind a Deity thus sublime and holy finds the life of every pure affection, and presses with omnipotent power on the conscience; and our only prayer is that we may walk as children of such light."

The heathen have no conception of God as a Father. The world sighs for fatherhood, and nothing less will satisfy the soul of man. The heart wants not a code of laws, not a system of doctrine, not a judge however just, not a bountiful provider and preserver, but a divine, sympathetic

Father. Philip's prayer, "Show us the Father, and it sufficeth us," is the orphan cry of humanity, the plaintive voice of the universal human heart. Nothing less can satisfy. And the search for God has been correctly characterized as the search for the principle of fatherhood. A great writer has truly said: " Without it [the doctrine of fatherhood] the religions of the West had perished amid license and apathy, while the more fervid spirits of the East took refuge in the thought of annihilation."

Next we will contrast Christianity and other religions in their *conceptions of man* and their estimates *of the value of human life.* This truth is axiomatic: the more exalted our conception of the God we worship, the nobler will be our estimate of man. Divine thoughts of God necessitate high thoughts of man. The greater the God whose lordship we recognize, and whose authority we obey, the greater the man created in his image or in any sense the representative of his character. Now in connection with this fundamental truth, though not necessarily deducible from it, I lay down these broad propositions: (1) Religions that do not believe in a personal God cannot believe in the divine origin, dignity, and individuality of man. Personality is instinct in man in proportion as the personality of God is distinct. (2) The doctrine of the immortality of man is conditioned on belief in the eternity of God. (3) Belief in the unity of man is not possible to those who believe in a multitude of gods. Polytheistic religions deny the unity of the human race, and its logical expression, the brotherhood of man.

These propositions are sustained and abundantly illustrated by the histories of the great non-Christian religions. Hindooism, which denies a personal God, does not recognize the existence of a real soul, but only a temporary emanation, like the moon's reflection in water. There is no capacity for fellowship, and the end is absorption.

From these low conceptions of the origin, dignity, and destiny of man there necessarily follows a cheap estimate of the value of human life. A life that has no future can have no value. We are not surprised, therefore, to find in all heathen countries contempt for human life. "China would see a thousand men perish with less concern than we would see a score." Until the strong arm of a Christian government prohibited it, human sacrifices were offered to their gods in India by the hundreds every year. Victor Hugo contrasted not only the sentiment of different civilizations, but the principles of antagonistic religions, in this sarcastic sentence: "If a man is killed in Paris, it is murder; the throats of fifty thousand people are cut in the East, and it is a question." Among the tribes of the South Seas human flesh was the cheapest food. James Calvert, the apostle of Fiji, tells of one wretched cannibal who was wont to put down a stone for every human body of which he partook, and his mound of horror reached the number of eight hundred and seventy-two stones.

Now contrast with these low ideas that degrade man, and make his existence of no more value than sheep in the shambles, the lofty conception of man's immortality and eternal personal identity introduced by Christianity—made in God's own image, capable of not only apprehending, but of having fellowship with the Divine, endowed with faculties that make him a partaker of the divine nature, and possessed of a personality distinct and deathless.

Christianity is the *only religion of redemption*. This is its preëminent characteristic. It is the approach of Heaven to man, that man may be lifted up to heaven. All heathen faiths are only "colossal systems of meritorious legalism." Hindooism has no Saviour and no salvation. It has no divine helper in hours of need, no mediator between fallen man and a holy God, and no regenerating spirit to create anew a nature stained with sin. Its only idea of ultimate redemption is a state of "absolute quiescence or the negation of all consciousness." And Buddhism recognizes only "a salvation which each man could gain for himself, and by himself, in this world, during this life, without the least reference to God or gods, either great or small." The most momentous question under Buddhism and Christianity has thus been contrasted: "The Christian inquirer asks, 'What shall I do to inherit eternal life?' the Buddhist, 'What shall I do to inherit eternal extinction?'" Buddha said, "The harvest I reap is Nirvana;" and Nirvana is annihilation. Jainism, a sect of Buddhism, teaches that man is perfected only after "myriads of births into this and other worlds," and by a long and painful process of penance and maceration. And the perfection at last attained is a state of "entirely unconscious repose." And Mohammedanism has no atonement. Salvation is by works only. The works prescribed in order to secure redemption are these: (1) *Prayer*, which is offered five times a day, with the face turned toward Mecca, accompanied by certain ablutions and purifications. (2) *Fasting*, which Mohammed called "the gate of religion."

(3) *Almsgiving*, the importance of which in their system was thus stated by a Moslem teacher of the early centuries: "Prayer carries us halfway to God, fasting brings us to the door of his palace, and alms procure us admission." (4) A pilgrimage to Mecca, which is an act of highest merit.

With these dreary responses to the bitter cry of burdened humanity, these Dead Sea apples pressed to the parched lips of the human soul, we contrast our Christian religion, with its blessed and inspiring promise of answered prayer and pardoned sin, and a purified nature, and an endless, sinless, joyous fellowship with the Son of God. It promises the infinite expansion of every power of the soul, and unending satisfaction to every stainless impulse. The enrapturing assurance is that each redeemed heart " shall be able to comprehend with all saints what is the breadth, and length, and depth, and height; and to know the love of Christ, which passeth knowledge, that he may be filled with all the fullness of God."

The two doctrines—that a sinless man was made sin, and that a dead and buried man was made life —Sir Monier Williams says makes a gulf between our Holy Bible and the so-called sacred books of the East, " which severs the one from the other utterly, hopelessly, and forever; not a mere rift across which the Christian and non-Christian may shake hands and interchange similar ideas in regard to essential truth, but a veritable gulf which cannot be bridged over by any science of religious thought; yes, a bridgeless chasm which no theory of evolution can ever span."

Heathen religions have no *high motives* and *lofty ideals*. With this low ethical aim and these despairing views of life there can be noble aspirations and inspired longings. There is nothing to kindle divine desire, nothing to exalt hope. When a personal God is denied and possible fellowship with him decried, there is nothing in a religion to satisfy pure desire; so the desire has to be annihilated. Buddhism is essentially repressive. It blasts and sterilizes the soil out of which springs nobility of character. Confucianism teaches men to beware of action and aim at inaction, indifference, and apathy as the highest of all states.

The difference between Buddhism and Christianity as motive powers has thus been stated: "Buddha so hated life as to extinguish the very desire to mend it; Christ so loved life as to create in all who loved him the desire for its ennoblement. The aim of Budhha was to make men know their misery, that they might be willing to lay down the burden of existence; but the purpose of Christ was to make men conscious of sin, that they might live unto holiness, forsake the darkness, and seek the light."

The images of Buddha, some of them of colossal proportions, represent the Oriental saint in a sitting posture and meditative mood, with hands folded and the palms upturned. The position of that figure of inaction and meditation is a fitting representation of the great system of religion of which he was the highest incarnation. It can produce nothing nobler than a type of character which is to mourn over the vanity of all things and sigh for Nirvana. A religion with such a contempt of life, and so entirely destitute of any spirit of aggression and enterprise, can never produce great characters or work out high plans for the world's uplifting.

Every missionary in every field and every tourist who has an eye to discern spiritual verities, agrees with Bishop Caldwell when he says: " I cannot imagine any person who has lived and moved among uneducated heathen in the rural districts believing them to be influenced by *high motives* in anything they do. They have never heard of such things as high motives, and cannot for a long time be made to comprehend what they mean." . It is true that Buddhism taught a form of self-sacrifice, which is said to be the foundation of the whole complex system; and of Buddha himself it is related that in one previous existence he plucked out his own eyes, and that in another he cut off his own head, and that in a third he cut his own body to pieces to redeem a dove from a hawk. But the distinction between the self-sacrifice taught by Buddhism and that inculcated and nobly illustrated by Jesus Christ is thus clearly set forth by Sir Monier Williams, probably the world's highest authority on that ancient religion: " Christianity demands the suppression of selfishness; Buddhism demands the suppression of self. In the one the true self is elevated and intensified; in the other the true self is annihilated by the practice of a false form of nonselfishness, which has for its final object the annihilation of the ego, the utter extinction of personal individuality."

Mohammedanism offers its worshipers not high moral and intellectual felicity, but "the everlasting gratification of their passions." Gratification of the lower nature becomes, therefore, the object of life. Its ethical system approves and encourages polygamy, divorce, and slavery, thus poisoning domestic life, degrading manhood, and disorganizing society. Individuality is absorbed into the life of the system, and all freedom of thought and right of private judgment entirely destroyed. As a matter of history, the legitimate result of such ethics and ignoble aims, non-Christian religions have developed no "creative personalities, no men who have originated and led great movements for the world's uplifting. They have produced no philanthropists and reformers and broad-minded patriots. Where are their John Howards and John Wesleys and George Washingtons? Out of such religions they can never be evolved. The highest expression of philanthropy in all India is hospitals for sick animals, inspired by their doctrine of transmigration. They will neglect afflicted men to care for a diseased dog, for in so doing they may be ministering to a dead son or daughter.

Contrast these dreary dreams of paganism with the lofty ideals and mighty motives of Christianity. Other religions have naught to live for but the present, and the present is considered essentially evil. All the motives of a great life are wanting. The future is but a dream at best. But how invigorating and inspiring are the ideals of Christianity! What exalted purposes to kindle aspiration! What noble enterprises to command our best endeavors! We are exhorted to nothing short of imitation of God himself. "Be ye imitators of God, as dear children."

Christianity exalts the meaning and mission of life. Its plans are projected into the eternal years. A man cannot rise above the object of his affection. Hence the exhortation, "set your affection upon things above, not on things on the earth." If the object of love is base and low, the man himself will be degraded to its level. If it is lofty and noble, he will be lifted up to its splendid nobility, however exalted. He cannot rise above his ideal. He rises or falls with the object of his supremest hope and affection. How striking is that picture John Bunyan drew of the old man with the muck rake in hand, bent low at his work, raking rotting weeds and leaves together; while just above him floated an angel, on radiant wing, with a crown in hand ready to place it upon his brow if he would only straighten up; but he never wore it, because he never looked up. He lost a crown by always looking down. That is a faithful picture of unsaved humanity everywhere, especially in heathen lands. A religion that has no lofty ideals—no hope in the future—and does not train the eye of the soul to look upward, has no "joy and crown." The sad angel may linger, poised on weary wing, but the hour of coronation will never come.

The unapproachable superiority of Christianity

is further shown in its *symmetrical development of human character*. And after all it is symmetry that gives beauty to character. It is formed not so much by "the gigantic size of one virtue," as by the harmony and completeness of all. Unlike national religions, with their limitations to the supposed needs of national life and their adaptations to national character, Christianity touches *humanity* at every point, and is adapted not only to all men, but to the *whole man*. There are no metes and bounds to its " exceeding breadth." It is not only " familiar with the chief notes of character, but also with those many semitones whose happy introduction makes the full music of moral perfection." There is not one appeal to one set of motives, and an ominous silence toward another; not a generous response to some cravings of the human heart, and a hard, closed hand to others equally urgent; but has an attentive ear for every cry of humanity—an unlimited supply for every need, ample reward for every effort, and an open, inviting field for the loftiest aspirations and the grandest achievements. The gentler and the sturdier virtues are alike developed. I thank Mr. Watkinson for this striking figure and eloquent passage: " The famous violin of the Hardanger region has its four delicate under-strings, whose vibrations add weird harmonies to the tones produced by the stroke of the bow on the four principal strings; so a nature developed and perfected by communion with Christ not only responds to the great appeals of common veracity and justice, but, full of the fine chords, makes all the delicate music which discerning souls know to be the music of the upper spheres."

Our religion contemplates the sanctification of the whole man, and is concerned with the entire range and round of life's activities and duties. "Whether therefore ye eat, or drink, or whatsoever ye do, do all to the glory of God." (1 Cor. x. 31.)

In his first Epistle to the Church at Thessalonica St. Paul thus prays: "And the God of peace himself sanctify you wholly; and may your spirit and soul and body be preserved entire, without blame at the coming of our Lord Jesus Christ. Faithful is he that calleth you, who will also do it."

All that is purest in purpose and holiest in life and tenderest in sympathy and sweetest in mercy and freest in charity and fairest in virtue and most beautiful in character are the direct inspiration of the Christian religion. But under no heathen system of religion or philosophy, even those with the largest element of truth, is it possible to develop a full-orbed character. At the best, "a man carries a catechism in his head and an arctic winter in his soul."

Christianity alone gives *comfort in bereavement.* Every other religion is pitiless. They have no voice to sympathize, no hand to soothe, no hope to cheer. Without a resurrection faith there is no cure for human sorrow. Nothing can be more utterly cheerless than the doctrine of the transmigration of souls: that our loved ones are reappearing in the forms of beasts and birds and fishes. One tradition is that Buddha himself had five hundred and fifty earlier lives before he became the son of Suddhodana. He had lived as a rat and a crow, as a frog and a hare, as a dog and a pig, twice as a fish, six times as a snipe, four times as a golden eagle, four times as a peacock and as a serpent, ten times as a goose, as a deer, and as a lion, six times as an elephant, four times as a horse and as a bull, eighteen times as an ape, four times as a slave, three times as a potter, thirteen times as a merchant, twenty-four times as a Brahman and as a prince, fifty-eight times as a king, twenty times as the god Indra, and four times as Mahabrahman. A believer in Jainism, who had suffered bereavement, was asked by a missionary if he hoped ever to see his dear one again. With a hopeless expression of countenance he replied: "How could I? My loved one is gone, gone forever!" No wonder the Hindoos burn their dead, for why should they keep a body whose spirit may at once become a frog or a crow? Hindooism has no graves. To their faith the stone can never be rolled from the door of the sepulcher, and the mortal form they loved never be clothed with immortality and given a glorified body. Hope never survives death. It ends all.

The highest hope of Buddhism is annihilation. It teaches that life is essentially evil, and escape therefrom the chief end of man. They hold, as Max Müller tells us, that "true wisdom consists in perceiving the nothingness of all things, and is a desire to become nothing, to be blown out, to enter Nirvana. . . . If to be is misery, not to be is felicity; and this felicity is the highest reward which Buddha promised to his disciples." And the heaven of Mohammedanism is nothing more than a "lustful paradise."

How incomparably more comforting and sustaining is our Christian religion! It has a balm for every wound, a comfort for every sorrow, and a joyful morning for every night of weeping. As contrasted with the dreadful doctrine of transmigration, how transfiguring is the assurance of heavenly recognition: that we shall know even as we are known!

Heathen religions have *no power to elevate*. Their highest aspiration is after nonexistence. They offer only a state of ease and sloth. Their heaven is an eternity of idleness or unconsciousness, as in Buddhism and Hindooism; or a "carnival of sensuous pleasure," as in Mohammedanism. Their gods *sleep*. All energy is emasculated and enterprise is treason to their ancestral faith. Hence Eastern nations are inert, slothful, apathetic; and this apathy is no less appalling than their immorality.

These religions debase manhood and degrade womanhood. No wonder a poor Hindoo woman, in sending a despairing appeal to Queen Victoria for some relief in India, closed with this agonizing prayer: "O God, I pray thee, let no more women be born in this land!"

The bells of Japan are tongueless. They have no power of melody within. By means of a large beam swung on ropes the ponderous bells are struck on the outside and made to wake the echoes of mountain and valley. And this I have thought most fitly represents the civilizations and religions of all the Orient. Dominated by a conservatism that produces stagnation, and their religions destitute of fellowship and hope, and therefore without inspiration, they have no capacity within themselves of elevating nations and making music for the march of the generations. But when struck from without—struck by the hammer of Christian truth, struck by the wand of Western enterprise, struck by the power of modern progress—chimes are awakened that charm the ear of nations and thrill the old lands themselves with the possibilities of a new and larger life. The late brilliant campaign of the Japanese against China—one splendid victory succeeding another with the rapidity of a drama, marching with almost unchallenged step from one conquered field to another—was really the majestic movement of Western ideas against the impassive and imperturbable Orient. The thunder of every Japanese gun hurled a projectile of Western thought. But all must come from without, and from the direct influence of Christian nations.

The only possible exception to the sterilizing influences of non-Christian religions is Mohammedanism; but those who speak by the authority of accurate and ample knowledge admit that it can only lift savage races up to a certain point (say to the Arabian civilization of the seventh century), and then " further progress is impossible except upon its absolute rejection." Mackey, of Uganda, speaks of the "strange venom" of Islam, and describes its votaries as "guilty of every form of uncleanness and robbery and tyranny and murder." I know of no more discriminating and just description of the genius, spirit, and influence of Mohammedanism than is to be found in these words from the pen of Bishop Alexander: "It once elevated the pagan Arabs. Even now it elevates the negro above his fetich; but it must ever remain a religion for stationary races, with its sterile god and its poor literality, the dead book pressing upon it with a weight of lead. Its merits are these: It inculcates a lofty, if sterile, theism; it fulfills the pledge conveyed in the word "Moslem" by inspiring a calm, if frigid, resignation to destiny; it teaches the duty of prayer with strange impressiveness; but whole realms of thought and feeling are crushed out by its bloody and lustful grasp. It is without purity, without tenderness, and without humility."

Mohammedanism has blighted every land it has touched. It is an absolute despotism, and crushes out the very life of nations. Founded on the principle of war, the resources of the countries are drunk up by its sword. It destroys accumulated wealth. It blasted Arabia, bankrupted Egypt, and exhausted Persia. Agriculture is discouraged by its frail land tenure. Look at Arabia, at Persia, at Turkey, at Egypt, at all Syria. Its history is a track of desolation and lamentation. It has no conservative forces.

But on the other hand Christianity has demonstrated itself to be the great character-developing and nation-uplifting force in the world. It gives dignity to labor, sanctity to marriage, nobility to woman, purity to domestic and social life, and promotes the brotherhood of man. It finds deserts and makes them gardens, trackless forests and converts them into fruitful fields, dreary marshes and builds great cities therein, hitherto unknown continents and establishes therein a higher civilization. What has been said of some countries will soon be said of every mission field: "Nations have been transformed; Christianity has become the law of the land; and idols, once in every house, have not been found, even as curios and relics! The adamantine wall of caste, the iron wheel of transmigration, the brazen fetters of Moslem bigotry, the hopeless thraldom of fetichism, have alike proved powerless to oppose the simple gospel of Christ." Everything lives whither the river cometh.

The marvelous progress of the world is limited to Christian nations. Account for it as others may, the astonishing fact remains that only in Christian countries is there any development, while in all heathen lands there is stagnation and decay. Now how is this progress to be explained? Why this strange coloring of the maps of the world? How happens it that the progressive and nonprogressive nations are differentiated by their attitude to Christianity?

Another fact distinguishing Christianity from other religions is *its attitude toward its Founder*. Christ, the center of the Christian system, is the supremest object of affection and adoration; the founders of other faiths may be revered, but are not loved. Confucius, the greatest philosopher of the East, is honored for his wisdom; but while his *words* are cherished, his person has no inspiration. Gautama, the founder of Buddhism, has not in himself any special charm to the votaries of that faith. Mohammed was a magnetic and intrepid leader, but only a prophet claiming to speak for the Lord. But in Christianity it is the person of Christ that has attractive and ennobling power. Christian loyalty is animated by personal affection; the heathen obeys through fear. The difference between Christian and heathen service is the difference between obedience and subservience. The Christian says, "O, how I love thy law!" the heathen says, "O, how I dread the gods!" What the venerable Dr. Legge says of the Chinese may be said with equal emphasis of the disciples of all heathen religions: "I have been reading Chinese books for more than forty years, and any general requirement to 'love God,' or the mention of any one as 'loving him,' has yet to come for the first time under my eye."

But in Christianity devotion to Jesus Christ is the source of all strength and the inspiration of every enduring form of heroism. In his "History of European Morals" Mr. Lecky pays this tribute to Christianity as a reforming and uplifting force in the world, the secret of which he discovers in the person of its great Founder: "It has been reserved for Christianity to present to the world an ideal character which through all the changes of eighteen centuries has filled the hearts of men with an impassioned love; has shown itself capable of acting in all ages, temperaments, and conditions; has not only been the highest pattern of virtue, but the highest incentive to its practice, and has exercised so deep an influence that it may be truly said that the simple record of three short years of Christ's active life has done more to regenerate and soften mankind than all the disquisitions of philosophers and all the exhortations of moralists.

It has been the wellspring of whatever is best and purest in the Christian life. Amid all the sins and failings, amid all the priestcraft and persecution and fanaticism that have defaced the Church, it has preserved in the character and example of its Founder an enduring principle of regeneration."

Paul, the great, calm thinker and apostolic leader, voiced at once his own ardent love for his Lord, and the sum of every true Christian's faith, when he exclaimed, "For me to live is Christ, and to die is gain;" and then, enraptured with the prospect of an eternal and uninterrupted personal fellowship, said that he desired "to depart, and to be with Christ; which is far better." The aged and sainted Polycarp, of Smyrna, when standing at the stake where his body was to be burned, and begged to recant that he might escape the flames, made answer in these brave words: "Eighty and six years have I been his servant, and he never did me an injury; how, then, can I blaspheme my King, who is my Saviour?" And similar testimony, in flame and blood, has been borne by multiplied millions. Dean Farrar says, with as much force as beauty: "It is strange and touching to see how this character, with the winning love of its irresistible tenderness, by the moral sorcery of its infinite self-sacrifice, pervades, astonishes, overwhelms, subdues."

But heathen religions have no such joyous spiritual fellowship and no such object of affection or encouragement to glorious endeavor. Their gods are as cold as an arctic winter, without love themselves, and unable to enkindle it in others. Speaking of the missionary Hionen—Thsang—called the St. Francis Xavier of Buddhism—who traveled once for four days and nights through a desert without a drop of water, Prof. Max Müller says: "He had nothing to refresh himself except his prayers, and what were they? Texts from a work which taught that there was no God, no Creator, no creation—nothing but mind, minding itself."

Of the Christ and his quiet conquests Jean Paul Richter says: "The lowliest among the mighty and the mightiest among the lowly, who with pierced hand has lifted the gates of empires off their hinges, turned the course of history out of its channel, and still governs the centuries."

Christianity is also distinguished from other religions by the *manner of its growth* and the *methods of its progress*. It proposes to conquer the world, but only by love. It marshals no armies and commands no navies and seeks to compel no people by force to surrender to the rule of the

King of kings. As Athanasius says, "No forced obedience pleases God. He dislikes that men should be made religious by hatchet and sword." And whenever misguided zealots have used the enginery of war or the power of civil government to advance the cause of Christ, the cause itself has suffered and the Spirit of the Lord has been grieved. The Word will win the world, "not by might, nor by power, but by my Spirit, saith the Lord of hosts." It advances by simple, gentle, unobtrusive means. As quiet as leaven, as soft as light, as persistent as salt, is the gospel of the kingdom "that cometh not with observation." It asks not the power of kings, nor the patronage of state, but only the privilege of simple proclamation and the miracle of holy living. These are the only means by which its conquest of the nations is to be achieved. Its victories have been won "not because of princes, but in spite of them." By heroic endurance, by burning zeal, by boundless love, the uttermost parts of the earth are to be possessed.

But no other faith has so won its way in the world. By the patronage of princes and the power of the sword every one has attained influence and wide acceptance. For centuries there was ceaseless conflict between Hindooism and Buddhism in India, and at last the latter had to cross the Himalayas and flee the country, leaving only a small following on the island of Ceylon. Shintoism is interwoven with the life of the State. And Mohammedanism is only another name for human cruelty and fanatical ferocity. The richest rewards and the most conspicuous places in the seventh heaven were promised those whose swords were wet with the blood of the largest number of infidels. In chapter xlvii. of the Koran are these words: "When ye encounter the unbelievers, strike off their heads, until ye have made a great slaughter among them. . . . O true believers, if ye assist God, by fighting for his religion, he will assist you against your enemies, and will set your feet fast; but as for the infidels, let them perish, and their works shall God render vain." Thus their hands were taught to war as the rarest virtue, and assuring the richest reward. Mohammed went so far as to say that "paradise rests under the shadow of swords." The difference between Christianity and Islam has thus been stated: "Converts were gained to the faith of Jesus by witnessing the constancy with which its confessors *suffered* death; they were gained to Islam by the spectacle of the readiness with which its adherents *inflicted* death. In the one case conversion often imperiled the believer's life; in the other, it was for the most part the only means of saving it."

And that spirit yet abides and gloats in blood. The atrocities of Armenia have appealed to the sympathy of the world, and a restraining hand has only been stayed by the fear of the greater horrors of a European war, in which every power would be involved. But Moslem fanaticism and inhumanity must go down before the peaceful triumphs of the Man of Galilee. It is true that the history of Christians under Moslem law "is only an uninterrupted scene of tyranny, violation, and slaughter;" but its civil power will soon be broken, and only linger as a hateful memory.

And another fact which shows the transcendent superiority of Christianity over other religions, is its *self-recuperative energy*. A divine religion must have the power of self-recuperation. If it wins by its inherent energy, it must organize victory even out of defeat. A religion is valueless that cannot meet a crisis. If dependent upon other and mightier influences for deliverance from peril or recovery from misalliance and mistake, it is shorn of any claim to be divine, and has forfeited all right and title to human confidence. Dependence is not a quality of divinity. If a religion has to be buttressed by supports, civil and secular, it is man-made, and not divine.

Christianity has never been aided, but rather hindered, by too close alliance with civil government. The kingdoms of Christ and Cæsar should be at peace, but *independent*. A striking illustration of the positive hurtfulness to Christianity by this forbidden union is the history of the church in connection with Constantine the Great. I adopt and reproduce the vigorously expressed opinion of Mr. Wesley thereon. He said: "Persecution never did, never could, give any lasting wound to genuine Christianity. But the greatest it ever received, the grand blow which was struck at the very root of that humble, gentle, patient love which is the fulfilling of the Christian law, the whole essence of true religion, was struck by Constantine the Great, when he called himself a Christian, and poured in a flood of riches and honor and power upon the Christians, more especially upon the clergy. I have been long convinced from the whole tenor of history that Constantine calling himself a Christian was productive of more evil to the Church than all the ten persecutions put together. From the time that the Church and the State, the kingdoms of Christ and of the world, were so strangely and unnaturally blended together,

Christianity and heathenism were so thoroughly incorporated with each other that they will hardly ever be divided until Christ comes to reign upon earth."

But out of all entanglements of false friends, and all embarrassments of misguided zeal, and all fierceness of persecution, Christianity comes by her own unaided effort, with a mightier vitality and a diviner glory. This recuperative and triumphant spirit of our holy religion dominates the very methods of the sacred writers even when pronouncing the judgments of God. Above the tones of lamentation there is always a voice of hope and the shout of final victory. Listen to Isaiah. Dark enough was the picture he drew of Israel's downfall, and dreadful were the judgments that he said were impending; but out of the gloom he sounded a note of cheer, " Behold, I lay in Zion for a foundation a stone, a tried stone, a precious corner stone, a sure foundation ;" and St. Paul, pained by the heresies he had to combat, and discouraged by so many apostasies from the true faith, until he is tempted to wonder if faith will still be found in the earth, yet cries out, with the notes of a bugle, "*nevertheless* the foundation of God standeth sure."

And Christianity never was so buoyant and aggressive as now. Every day marks a notable advance. Through flame and flood and blood the gospel has come, and moves onward with a steadier and statelier step to the conquest of the nations. Nothing can stay its conquering course. "No despotism can ever destroy or permanently arrest the gospel, because it has the light of God upon it and the life of men within it."

The age is remarkable for eager inquiries into the life and person of Christ. All peoples are face to face with the question: "What think ye of Christ?" He is the theme of poet, the study of philosopher, the model of artist, the teacher of statesmen, the inspiration of philanthropist, the friend of the poor, and the brother of every man. It is said to have required four large volumes to record simply the names and contents of the books that have been written concerning the person of Christ. Mr. Gladstone says: "Talk about the questions of the day: there is but one question, and that is the gospel of Christ. It can and will correct everything needing correction."

But while Christianity triumphs, every other religion is failing. They are toppling to their utter ruin. Enfeebled with years, they are without power to renew their youth like the eagle. Their vitality is decaying, with nothing to arrest the process of death. Their most sacred shrines are neglected, and venerable temples are crumbling. A waning crescent, Moslems themselves admit, fitly foretells their future. In the published accounts of the burning of the famous mosque at Damascus a few years ago there was a suggestive coincidence, if not a striking prophecy. It was built on the sacred spot where once stood the old Byzantine Church, dedicated to St. John the Baptist. In building this Moslem temple one of the Roman arches was blended in the superstructure, on which was a Greek inscription from the Holy Scriptures. After the great fire the arch was found in place, bending over the ruins, bearing these words: "Thy kingdom, O Christ, and thy dominion endureth throughout all ages."

The distinguished Boden Professor of Sanscrit at Oxford, probably the best authority, says that "as a form of popular religion Buddhism is gradually losing its vitality and hold on the vast populations once loyal to its rule." He computes the number of Buddhists at one hundred million, not four hundred million, as hitherto estimated; and gives the first place numerically to Christianity. The order, according to number of adherents, is as follows: Christianity, Confucianism, Hindooism, Buddhism, Mohammedanism.

There is a painting in the Vatican gallery repre

senting *paganism in prophecy*. It is a broken column, which has fallen, and is partly covered with sand and weeds. However long it may have stood in stately strength, at last it falls, and is being fast buried out of sight. The picture is true to life. History is rapidly fulfilling that prophecy. Throughout the world the power of paganism is broken, and sooner or later will be covered under the sweep and growth of the centuries.

But I have another picture in mind—a figure of Christianity—not in dead stone, but in living nature. I find it in an account of a mysterious tree in the old city of Canton, China. It grows on the ruins of an ancient pagoda, and is green all the year round. From what source it draws its vigorous and beautiful life is something of a mystery. Other leaves turn sear and yellow, but these seem never to fade. On the crumbling *débris* of that old, decaying pagoda, the tree waves aloft its green branches like another angel of the resurrection, proclaiming its independence and defiance of the whole empire of death. That is God's prophecy in a figure. On the ruins of Confucianism, Buddhism, Hindooism, and every doomed religion, there has been planted the tree of life, whose leaves are for the healing of the nations, and which beareth its fruit in all seasons.

CHRISTIANITY AND OTHER RELIGIONS. 75

I conclude, therefore, this discussion with the eloquent exhortation of Sir Monier Williams, whose profound knowledge of other religions has only intensified his appreciation of the absolute truth of the Christian system and strengthened his faith in its ultimate and glorious triumph. He says:

Go forth, then, ye missionaries, in your Master's name; go forth into all the world, and, after studying all its false religions and philosophies, go forth and fearlessly proclaim to suffering humanity the plain, the unchangeable, the eternal facts of the gospel; nay, I might almost say the stubborn, the unyielding, the inexorable facts of the gospel. Dare to be downright with all the uncompromising courage of your own Bible, while with it your watchwords are love, joy, peace, reconciliation. Be fair, be charitable, be Christlike, but let there be no mistake. Let it be made absolutely clear that Christianity cannot, must not, be watered down to suit the palate of either Hindoo, Parsee, Confucianist, Buddhist, or Mohammedan; and that whosoever wishes to pass from the false religion to the true can never hope to do so by the rickety planks of compromise, or by the help of faltering hands held out by half-hearted Christians. He must leap the gulf in faith, and the living Christ will spread his everlasting arms beneath, and land him safely on the eternal Rock.

LECTURE III.

PORTABLE EVIDENCES FROM MANY LANDS.

III.

PORTABLE EVIDENCES FROM MANY LANDS.

IN this lecture I shall consider what has been happily called "the portable evidences" of Christianity—the testimony of those in different lands and reared under various religions who have put *our* religion to an experimental test and have become "living epistles" of its redeeming virtue and power. Christianity claims to produce certain results wherever and whenever embraced by individuals and peoples. It only asks to be tested by a spiritual trial of its divine energy. Indeed, it seeks every opportunity of making demonstration of its infinite power. And after all, a spiritual experience is the final evidence. Slightly modified, I adopt the words of Thomas Carlyle: To *test* religion, and "to 'teach' religion, the first thing needful, and also the last and the only thing, is the finding of a man who *has* religion." A living Lazarus, who has been four days dead, is the convincing answer to all cavil. He is the absolute demonstration of resurrection power. Bishop Westcott thus clearly states the case: "The verification of the gospel is in and through life, the life of men, and the life of each man. It is verified outwardly by the testimony of history; it is verified inwardly by the testimony of experience."

Now it is boldly affirmed that Christianity extends, without distinction, "to all men, to the whole of man, to all being and to all time," and that it is entirely adequate to meet the needs of all men, and is perfectly adapted to every possible human condition. Of course, such a claim must be supported by evidence. But if men in different lands and latitudes, in every stage of civilization and intelligence, and reared under various philosophies and religions, from the highest Buddhism to the lowest fetichism of the South Sea Islands, embrace Christianity and bear the same testimony to its saving and sanctifying power, we are justified in accepting the universality of its adaptation and mission—its perfect correspondence "with the original constitution and the actual condition of man."

Our Lord certainly had a vision of world-wide empire. He purposed nothing less than a universal and everlasting kingdom. His command, therefore, is "to preach the gospel to every creature" —no limit of territory, race, caste, class, or condition. And the promise is that "all shall know the Lord, from the least to the greatest." And that command is based upon the possibility of universal redemption and the pledge of His exhaustless resources to achieve it. The supposition is that no such command would have been given, if men were not able to receive it. Now we claim that the history of modern Missions has converted that conclusion into a demonstration. It has demonstrated the capacity of man, everywhere, to apprehend Christian truth. He may not be able to understand the metaphysics of theology; but the spiritual verities of the gospel, which renew the life and mold the character, can be apprehended and reincarnated by *all men*.

This broad statement is supported by two considerations:

1. Enlightenment of the heart, rather than the head, is the condition of spiritual knowledge. The heart has eyes. St. Paul speaks of "having the eyes of your heart enlightened." This inner eye, opened, is the organ of spiritual discernment. Now it is much the same in all men. The affectionate nature and the natural conscience are on the same level among all races and nations. There are vast differences in intellectual capacity and culture, but the natural heart is quite the same. Jeremy Taylor makes this discriminative observation: "Every man understands more of religion by *his affections* than by his reason. It is not the

wit of man, but the spirit of the man; not so much his head as his heart that learns the divine philosophy." Our Lord was therefore eminently philosophical when he said: " Blessed are the pure in heart: for *they* shall see God."

But this in no sense discounts the intellect, or underrates the right use of reason in religion. All religion worthy the homage of the heart must have an intellectual basis. Knowledge furnishes the materials of faith. A distinguished German writer said: " By my faith, I am a Christian; by my reason, I am a heathen." On that covert sneer Dr. Fairbairn makes this just observation: "Any theory that leaves a division in a man's own soul is false. If religion be a mere matter of faith, unable to bear the light of reason, it is untrue to the nature the Creator gave to man."

2. The other consideration is that obedience is also a condition of spiritual knowledge. David, therefore, spoke of himself not boastfully, but philosophically, when he said: " I have more understanding than all my teachers, *because I keep thy commandments.*" So our Lord says: " If any man will do his will, he shall know of the doctrine, whether it be of God, or whether I speak of myself." And there is earnest and repeated exhortation to " taste and see that the Lord is good."

But before calling the witnesses from many lands, and of every color of skin and former habit of life to bear testimony to the regenerating power of Christianity in their own lives—to speak by the authority of their own personal experience—it may be well to define Christian experience, and consider what is the value of such testimony. "Experience," as defined by the lexicographers, is "particular acquaintance with any matter by personal observation or trial of it; by feeling its effects; by living through it." As applied to the Christian religion it is, in a word, consciousness of certain internal states and feelings, through which one has passed or is passing. Schleiermacher said that religion is not a system of dogmas, but an "inward experience."

Now, such testimony—the testimony of consciousness—is most valuable. "Behind consciousness one cannot go; as far back as consciousness religion must go, or its work is superficial." It is "the affidavit of life to life." About every important event in history there may be somewhat varying accounts as to details. These, however, do not impeach, but rather confirm, the reliability of testimony. But, as Dr. Harrison has well said, "If there is one moral fact that is capable of absolute demonstration, it is the soul's attitude toward its Creator. . . . It is possible to demonstrate to the consciousness of man both his need of a Saviour and the presence of the Saviour that is needed." On the reliability of experience Leibnitz says: "If our immediate internal experience could possibly deceive us, there could no longer be for us any truth of fact; nay, nor any truth of reason." And Herbert Spencer himself admits the demonstration of experiences of this character in this luminous sentence: "When . . . the postulate is . . . not based on one concrete experience, . . . but *implies* an induction from a great variety of experiences, we may say that it *ranks next to the postulates of exact science.*"

And in this connection I ask you to delay yet a moment, in order to call attention to an important distinction, suggested by Bishop Foster, that "there is a difference between *an experience of Christianity* and *a Christian experience.*" The one is an observation of its moral, social, and other effects upon individuals, peoples, and nations; while the other is purely subjective—the consciousness of certain spiritual facts, forces, and fruits in the individual soul. One, therefore, may have an experience of Christianity—may have extensive and even approving knowledge of its mighty objective influences and results—and yet be without a genuine Christian experience. Sir William Muir, once Lieutenant Governor of the Northwest Provinces, had an experience of Christianity, but not necessarily a Christian experience, when, in referring to the increased ratio of conversions, he said: "And they are not shams or paper converts, as some would have us believe, but good, honest Christians, and many of them of a high standard." And so the Governor of Madras, a few years ago, had an experience of Christianity when he reported that in justice to those nations that had adopted Christianity as their profession in India, he ought not to refrain from bearing his testimony to that which came more especially under the eyes of a Governor—viz., their conduct in civil matters as well as their conduct in religious matters. When they come to large masses of his people, to whole villages which had adopted Christianity, then it was possible to those in authority to form some opinion as to whether the change of creed had conduced to the good conduct of the converts; and he must not refrain from saying that the tendency of the change had been decidedly good. And the native Prince of Travancore, though avowedly not a Christian, had an experience of Christianity, and thus publicly stated the results of his observations:

Where did the English-speaking people get all their intelligence and energy and cleverness and power? It is their Bible that gives it to them. And now they bring it to us and say: "This is what raised us." They do not force it upon us, as the Mohammedans did their Koran; but they bring it in love, and translate it into our languages, and lay it before us, and say: "Look at it, read it, examine it, and see if it is not good." Of one thing I am convinced: Do what we will, oppose it as we may, it is the Christian Bible that will, sooner or later, work the regeneration of this land. Marvelous has been the effect of Christianity in the moral molding and leavening of Europe. I am not a Christian; I do not accept the cardinal tenets of Christianity as they concern man in the next world; but I accept Christian ethics in their entirety. I have the highest admiration for them.

Another fact should not be overlooked: While the attitude of regenerated souls is essentially the same toward God and the great verities of the gospel, "every experience is colored by the subject of the experience." Inherited tendencies, degrees of intelligence, peculiarities of temperament, former habits, and, indeed, everything that differentiates human beings, affect and determine the expressions of this new life. Mental and temperamental characteristics are untouched in regeneration. Individuality is preserved. So in Christian experience, "every bird sings according to its beak." But there are certain great, radical results wrought in every one who accepts and, with the heart, believes these great truths. These are facts of consciousness to which he testifies, and as they affect life and conduct become facts of observation.

Now in listening to the testimonies of native Christians, recently emerged from heathenism, and studying the character of converts in the various mission fields, three suggestions are offered for our guidance:

' 1. Of necessity there must be immaturity of thought and character. The inheritors of centuries of ignorance and superstition cannot escape the period of spiritual and moral infancy.

2. We must acknowledge that there have been discouraging lapses in the mission fields. Not every convert has been faithful to his new profession. In a few instances whole communities have lapsed into heathenism. The break with old faiths was never complete. A man in the New Hebrides, for several years a professor of Christianity, was discovered, after his death, to have retained three sacred stones with which to raise storms, make rains, and bring disease. At Delhi, in India, almost one entire mission returned to heathen rites. That these lapses should occur is not surprising. The poison of superstition transmitted through the centuries, and the tyrannous social ostracisms which men of weak courage are unable to withstand, may easily account for them. We won-

der that so few fail, that so many are steadfast. But so it has ever been. The parable of the sower is at once the picture of all lands and the history of the gospel in all countries and centuries. Some seed fall where there is not much depth of earth. The greatest trial of St. Paul's faith was the infidelities of professed disciples. On one occasion he said with a sad heart: "Demas hath forsaken me." Again: "All in Asia have turned aside from me." Often he had to lament the falling away of those from whom he had a right to expect generous support and valued service.

It is no impeachment of the integrity of Christianity, and no underrating of its saving, sanctifying power, that all its *professed* disciples are not saints; that some are defective in character, untrustworthy in conduct, and positively traitorous in spirit. Every system must be measured by its best products, by its noblest results. A criminal who defies law, outrages public morals, and suffers the penalty of his guilt, is not a fair representative of our Christian civilization. He is the condemnation, and not the commendation, of our national life; the refuse, and not the representative, of our public opinion. We do not go to the records of our criminal courts, to our prisons and scaffolds, to find the flower of American manhood and womanhood.

There is not found the proper standard by which to measure the value and virtue of our social institutions. We must look into our American homes, where honor and integrity dwell, and read the stories of heroism, patriotism, and piety that adorn the annals of our country, if we would have a true conception of the spirit and power of our national institutions.

What, then, we ask, can Christianity do in developing character out of the materials and circumstances of human life? What are the legitimate products of its ethics and its religion? Who are the proper representatives of its graces and virtues?

In the New Testament these graces find illustration in such beautiful characters as the apostle John, and not in the traitorous conduct of an Iscariot; the splendid heroism of St. Paul, and not in the cunning of an Alexander the coppersmith or the duplicity of a Simon Magus.

Because Balaam was a false prophet did not the Lord have any voice whom the people could trust? Were there no loyal souls in all Israel on whose lips God had placed a live coal from off his high altar? There were unworthy priests who plundered the sanctuary, made merchandise of their office, and burned strange fire before the Lord. But for every one that was false and faithless there were a hundred who had clean hands and pure hearts and clear discernment to know what Israel ought to do. And so through the ages the Church has suffered from unworthy friends, but God has ever had brave and true prophets to be his voice to the nations.

3. We must also take into account the immense strain upon one's fidelity and firmness to become a Christian in a heathen land. In a country where Christianity is the dominant sentiment there is little or no courage in confessing Christ. On the contrary, there may be social embarrassment and political ostracism because of avowed infidelity. It may be true, as averred, that blatant skepticism in our country has shut the door of high political preferment in the face of some who might otherwise have entered in. Now, if these things could occur in a land of such intellectual, religious, and political tolerance, what might we not expect in the narrow, fanatical, and autocratic countries of the East. Attachment to Christianity means detachment from everything personally and socially dear in life. Every open disciple becomes an outcast. The confession of Christ means not only "exile, poverty, persecution, contempt, but impiety to their ancestors, treason to their country, sacrilege to their gods."

To the character of native converts in India this positive testimony is from one who has authority to speak: "If deep repentance, earnest faith, and burning love; if complete self-sacrifice is a cheerful surrender of all that men hold dear in life; if a fearless confession of Christ at any cost be marks of genuine conversion, then has the Church of India multitudes of confessors within her pale distinguished by these marks."

And like strong witness is given in a report of the Darjeeling Mission: . . . "If the inevitable cross of baptism and discipleship, involving not unfrequently the loss of all the natural man counts dear, and involving always the surrender of cherished evil habits—if favorable comparison with the best Churches of Christendom, in respect of quotable instances of pious lives and pious deaths, the proportion of enrolled communicants and active workers' attendance on ordinances, zeal for education, Christian liberality, mutual benevolence, freedom from vice and crime—if all this is any test of sincerity, they are preëminently sincere, and we may rest reasonably satisfied regarding them."

But our purpose is not to ascertain the observations of others upon the Christian character of mission converts; we are to listen to their own statements as to the power of the gospel in their hearts and lives. The experiences to be related and the characters rapidly sketched are only a few of many that might be given from the vast volume of testimony at command; but these show how unsatisfactory are all the false faiths of the world, and are a triumphant vindication of Christianity's perfect adaptation to all classes of mind, all stages of civilization, and all conditions of humanity. The characters are introduced without reference to chronology or country.

Joseph Neesima.

Joseph Neesima, the first native apostle of Japan, would rank as a remarkable man of highest culture in the most golden age. We wonder that an inheritor of centuries of superstition and idolatry could not only have such clear spiritual apprehension of Christian truth, but should have so thoroughly mastered its theology, and expounded it with such critical scholarship. His character was as symmetrical as his gifts were remarkable. In him "reason and religion ran together like warp and woof to weave the web of a holy life."

Born of honorable parents, in the home of a prince, to whom his father was secretary, he was just ten years old when Commodore Perry anchored his flagship in the Bay of Yeddo. Early taught to worship the family gods on the shelf, and made acquainted with the Confucian classics, he was a Shintoist of the straitest sect. But a copy of a Chinese Bible which he chanced to see one day at the home of a friend opened wide the inquiring mind of the brilliant youth. He ceased to worship idols. From the conception of God as Creator, he soon recognized him as his Heavenly Father, and then, said he, "I discovered for the first time that the doctrines of Confucius on the filial relation were too narrow and fallacious." So from the religious and social systems of his country, though it cost the sacrifice of home and friends for years, he broke away, because they failed to satisfy the quest of his mind and the hunger of his soul.

By a chain of strange providences he came to America, under the patronage of Mr. Joseph Hardy, of Boston; was educated at Amherst and Andover, became a devout Christian, and returned to his native land to found a Christian university and be to Japan a second St. Paul. The text most frequently quoted in his journal was, "For God so loved the world that he gave his only begotten Son, that whosoever believeth in him should not perish, but have everlasting life," of which in later years he said: "This verse is the sun among all the stars which shine upon the pages of God's holy Word." On the opposite page in his journal is this prayer: "O Lord, wash away my sins, take up my evil heart, and give me the right spirit to understand and remember thy holy Word more and more. O God, wilt thou help me to destroy many gods and idols? Please destroy them with thy power, and let me be comforted," etc.

He was asked by the Japanese Minister at Washington to return to Japan and establish schools there after the American system. Of that visit and request of the high official he thus wrote: "When I saw the Japanese Minister at Amherst I told him that I would not go home concealing my Christian faith like a trembling thief goes in the dark night under the fear of discovery, but go there as a Christian man, walking in Christian love, and doing things according to the light of my conscience."

When about ready to return to his native land and aid in its evangelization, his eager soul caught a glimpse of the open field, and he cried out: "I feel that my active battlefield has come within my sight. I am ready to march forward, not asking whether my powder is dried or not, but trusting simply and believing only that the Lord of hosts will help me to do my duty." Again, in language almost equal to the sublime declaration of Moses, ne said: "I would rather preach or teach the truth which is in Christ Jesus with the bread of affliction than to do other things with the earthly luxuries, pleasures, and honors."

On his return he was the divinely commissioned instrument of his aged father's clear conversion to Christianity, and of turning a heathen house into a Christian home. He founded a great university at Kioto and gave it the suggestive name of "Doshisha," meaning "*One Purpose* or *One Endeavor Company.*" Within those walls he saw over nine hundred fine young men gathered, breathing a wholesome Christian atmosphere, and receiving the impress of his own sanctified genius. He was in labors most abundant. His quenchless zeal consumed his frail body. Divine impatience for the redemption of his people exhausted his vital energies. In an appeal for help to extend his work, he thus wrote between his tears: "My heart is constantly burning like a volcanic fire for my dearly beloved Japan. Pray for me, that I may rest in the Lord."

In an impassioned argument in favor of a quickened step and a grand forward movement, he flung out these words, that ring like the notes of a bugle, and ought to be the lofty motto of every Christian soldier: "WE MUST ADVANCE ON OUR KNEES." And in the midst of busy planning, the maps of all the provinces spread out before him, he fell asleep, with these words trembling from his lips: "Peace, joy, heaven." The story of that great scholar, educator, statesman, saint, and apostle is one of the most brilliant in all the annals of spiritual chivalry. If Christianity can lift one Japanese from the cheerlessness of Shintoism and the frigid philosophy of Confucianism into the dignity and glory of such a character, why can it not save the whole nation, making each subject of the Mikado a citizen of the kingdom of Christ? It can—and it will.

JOEL BULU'S EXPERIENCE.

This man, a native of the Friendly Islands, and brought to a knowledge of Christ through the agency of the Wesleyan missionaries, was for forty years a consistent Christian and a tireless missionary among the Fijians. For clearness of spiritual apprehension and the joyousness of a conscious salvation through faith in Christ, his experience is above the average in the Church at home. This is his own statement, translated by a missionary:

> I was born in Vavan in the heathen days, nor was it till I was a big lad that the *lotu* [their word for the "new religion"] came to our land. When I heard the report of it I was full of anger, and my soul burned with hatred against it. "And shall our gods be forsaken?" I cried in great wrath. "As for me, I

will never forsake them." One day I heard a man talking of the *lotu*, who said that it promised a land of the dead different from the *bulotu* of which our fathers spoke, even a home in the sky for the good, where evil men were cast into a dreadful place, wherein there burned a fire which none could quench. On that very night I went forth with the lads of the town—it was a fine night—and, looking up to the heavens where the stars were shining, this thought suddenly smote me, "O the beautiful land! If the words be true which were told us to-day, then are these *lotu* people happy indeed;" and my soul longed with a great longing to reach that beautiful land. I could not rest, so I went to another town, where dwelt a Christian chief, to tell him that I wished to *lotu*. "Good is your coming," cried the chief, and great was his joy. "But why do you want to *lotu?*" "I have heard," was my reply, "of the good land whither you go after death; therefore do I wish to *lotu*, that I also may be a dweller in the sky." So they prayed over me, and thus it was that I turned to Christianity; but of its meaning I knew nothing. Then came Mr. Thomas to Vavan, and, standing under a tree in the public square, he preached to us from the parable of the tares among the wheat. It was this sermon that pierced my soul; for I had thought that I was one of the wheat, but now I found that I was among the tares. As I heard I wept and trembled, for I thought: " I shall never see the good land." When the sermon was over and the people rose to go I sat in my place quaking for fear and weeping in great anguish, for all the strength had gone out of my body. "What is the matter with you?" they asked. "Pray for me, pray for me, I beseech you!" So they knelt down and prayed for me, first one and then another, till they were tired, but I found no comfort. So I rose, and, going into an empty outhouse, I knelt down there by myself, weeping and praying before the Lord, for now I felt that I was a sinner;

the wrath of God lay heavy upon my soul, and I hated myself because of my evil ways. "O what is that repentance whereof the preacher told us?" I cried; "Lord, let me find it, that I may live!" for so dark was my mind that I did not know that this sorrow and fear of mine were marks of repentance. Thus I continued a long while seeking the Lord in prayer with many tears.

At last there came a day, in 1834, when the missionaries (of whom Mr. Turner was one) assembled us together to hold a love feast; and when we had sung a hymn and prayed, then Mr. Turner stood up to declare the work of God in his soul. My heart burned within me as I listened to his words, for in speaking of himself he told all that I had felt, and I said to myself: "We are like two canoes sailing bow and bow, neither being swifter nor slower than the other." Thus it was with me when he told of his repentance; but when he went on to speak of his faith in Christ, the forgiveness of his sins, and the peace and joy which he had in believing, then said I: "My mast is broken, my sail is blown away; he is gone clear out of my sight, and I am left here drifting helplessly over the waves." But while I listened eagerly to his words, telling of the love of Christ to him, my eyes were opened; I saw the way, and I, even I, also believed and lived. I was like a man fleeing for his life from an enemy behind him, and groping along the wall of a house in the dark to find the door that he may enter in and escape, when lo! a door is suddenly opened before his face, and straightway, with one bound, he leaps within. Thus it was to me as I listened to the words of Mr. Turner; my heart was full of joy and love, and the tears streamed down my cheeks. Often had I wept before, but not like my former weeping were the tears which I now shed. Then I wept out of sorrow and fear, but now for very joy and gladness, and because my heart was full of love to Him who had loved me and given himself for me;

and Mr. Turner, seeing the tears raining heavily down from my eyes, called upon me to speak. "Stand up, Joel," said he, "and tell us how it is with you." So I stood up; but it seemed to me as if my soul were parted from my body, and I remembered nothing more until I found myself lying on the mat, and the missionaries weeping over me, and saying: "What is this?" "I live," said I, "I live. Let me rise, that I may declare the mercies of God." And even while I spoke there arose a great cry in our midst, and a burst of weeping, for the hearts of all were strangely moved. O what a day was that! Never can I forget it. The prayers, the praises, and the tears of joy!"

AFRICANER.

The name of Robert Moffat is indissolubly connected with Africaner, the first convert of his ministry, once a bloodthirsty chief of a cruel tribe, and then one of the humblest and gentlest followers of the meek and lowly Man of Galilee. The miracle of grace that converted this wild Namaqua warrior into a Christian brother and hero was in all respects equal to that which transformed the persecuting Saul of Tarsus into Paul, the greatest of the apostles. Ferocious even to wolfishness, and rapacious almost beyond comparison, he was a tyrant and a terror. His name was the synonym of all that was cruel and terrible. Neighboring chiefs and their tribes fled affrighted at the very report of his coming. But under the ministry of Robert Moffat this monster of cruelty became the gentlest of brothers. His heart opened to the truth, Christ was apprehended by faith, the pardoning voice of God was heard, and a new song was put into his mouth. Through the centuries this story of Africaner's marvelous transformation will linger in all South Africa as a memorial and a testimony. Of him, as of Saul of Tarsus, it might be said: "There fell from his eyes as it had been scales; and he received sight forthwith, and arose, and was baptized." And as the brethren at Jerusalem, on Saul's first return, "were all afraid of him, and believed not that he was a disciple," so the Dutch farmers and others at first refused to believe that Africaner could become a Christian; but when they saw and heard him, lifted high their hands and exclaimed: "This is the eighth wonder of the world! Great God, what a miracle of thy power and grace!" His entire after life was in perfect accord with this transforming experience of the Spirit. His ferocity was turned into spiritual fervor, and his rapacity into a consuming zeal "for God and his missionary." He became Moffat's protector and provider. He built him a house, provided other comforts, was his watchful and tender nurse in a critical illness, and accompanied him with a body-guard on a visit to Cape Town when he had reason to fear that the brave missionary's life might be in peril. In the home land there was never a more devout worshiper in the sanctuary or a more eager and prayerful student of God's word.

When he discovered that his health was failing, and apprehended that the end was not far off, he gathered his chief men about him and delivered a solemn charge. He said: "We are not now what we once were—*savages*—but men professing to be taught according to the gospel. Let us then do accordingly." Then he counseled them with great tenderness to be peaceful, brotherly, united, devoted to God, and ever to extend the largest hospitality to all Christian missionaries.

It has been said of this, his dying confession, that it "would have graced the lips of the Apostle of the Gentiles:" "I feel that I love God, and that he has done much for me of which I am totally unworthy. My former life is stained with blood; but Jesus Christ has bought my pardon, and I am going to heaven. Beware of falling into the same evils into which I have so often led you; but seek God, and he will be found of you and direct you." Having thus finished his course, Africaner fell asleep, leaving an imperishable memorial of the power of God unto salvation.

Ling Ching Ting, the Converted Opium Smoker.

This man, at forty years of age, strayed into a street chapel at Ato, a suburb of Foochow, in 1863, and heard a sermon by Rev. S. L. Brinkley. He listened with close attention, and lingered after service to talk with the missionary. "Did you say that Jesus (I never heard of him before; I don't know who he is); but did you say that he can save me from my sins?" "Yes," replied the missionary, "that is just what I said." "But," the Chinaman responded, "you didn't know me when you said that; you didn't know that I had been a gambler and sorcerer for many years; you didn't know that I had been a licentious man; you didn't know that I had been an opium smoker for twenty years, and every one knows that a man who has smoked opium for that length of time can never be cured of the habit. If you had known all this, you wouldn't have said that Jesus can save me from all my sins— would you?" "Yes," replied the missionary, "I would have said just what I did; and I tell you now that Jesus can save you from all your sins."

He was deeply perplexed. He went away and returned next day, and from day to day came to examine proofs of Christianity, bringing his objections to be answered. But one day he came with radiant countenance, and exclaimed: "I know it! I know it! I know that Jesus can save me from my sins, for he has done it."

He conquered the opium habit, and became an earnest evangelist. His words were with power. He went to Hok-Chiang to preach, when at length he was arrested on false charges, brought before a corrupt district magistrate, and sentenced to be beaten with two thousand stripes. The cruel sentence was executed with bamboo on his bare back. He was carried to the mission premises in Foochow, more dead than alive. When the missionary came into his room he said: "Teacher, this poor body is in great pain just now; but my inside heart has great peace. Jesus is with me; and I think perhaps he will take me to heaven, and I will be glad to go." Then the old fire began to flash in his eyes, and, raising himself a little, he added: "But if I get up from this, you'll let me go back to Hok-Chiang, won't you?"

After a long time he recovered and resumed his evangelistic work with consuming zeal. For fourteen years he was in labors most abundant, lived a blameless life, endured persecution, and died in triumph.

Hok-Chiang, where he was so cruelly treated, became a fruitful field. In 1890 there were seven hundred members, five hundred probationers, and over fifteen hundred adherents. Thus the works of the brave evangelist do follow him. The converted Buddhist became a flaming apostle.

A Japanese Judge.

Among the members of the East Osaka Methodist Church is a judge of the Appeal Court, who for many years has occupied high judicial position. He is an earnest Christian, and recently has become so burdened in spirit for the evangelization of his native land as to tender his resignation as a judge, that he may devote himself, at his own charges, to the salvation of his people. The letter, addressed to his pastor, Rev. W. E. Towson, announcing his purpose, has just been made public. It indicates the Pauline spirit. A few extracts are here given:

> I was baptized and converted to Christianity in 1890; and now, as I look over our country, strong impressions come to my heart. Our country is zealously adopting Western civilization from about thirty years ago, such as railway, telegraph, medical science, law, military, navy, politics, etc. We are very happy to live at this day, but I regret that the people do not come to the light of Christ, except some few persons. Evangelization is very necessary for Japan. Judge is worldly work, and there are very many candidates; but evangelist is religious

service, and there are very few candidates. I think I can be more useful to our country to work as an evangelist than to serve as a judge, and it is with rejoicing that I have resolved to do so after serious consideration.

1. I believe that the Lord has chosen me to do some work for the evangelization of Japan.

2. I intend to work as a free evangelist and to preach the gospel in a self-supporting way.

3. I have served as a judge for fifteen full years, and so am due a small pension, which will barely support my family.

4. When I need more money than my pension I will work as a lawyer.

5. A judge is not allowed to preach in public, but a lawyer can do so.

6. I think that one can change his profession when he has full conviction that he is called to a higher work. Many of the Lord's disciples have left their profession to work for Jesus. I feel as Paul did: "Woe is unto me, if I preach not the gospel."

First Native Bishop of the Niger, Samuel Adjai Crowther.

One of the miracles of Missions, and one of the most remarkable of "living epistles"—was Samuel Adjai Crowther, the first native Bishop of the Niger. Born in 1808, converted at the age of seventeen, and thence to the end of his days a blameless and fearless apostle of Christ, he illustrated as have few men the wonder-working power of divine grace. At twelve years of age Mohammedan marauders overran his country, killed his father, and carried the boy into slavery. He was traded for a horse, separated from his mother, and taken to the coast, where the Portuguese had anchored their slave ships. With one hundred and eighty-six others he was crowded into the hold of a vessel, and started westward; but the slave ship was given chase by two English men-of-war and captured, and the human beings in irons were landed at Sierra Leone. Here the slave boy, Adjai, was taken to a mission school, and there he was joyously converted to God and baptized as Samuel Crowther. He became first a pupil, then a teacher, in Yoruba Bay College. He translated the Scriptures into the Yoruba dialect, prepared a dictionary of the Yoruba tongue, besides many other books.

On his several visits to England he pleaded the cause of African missions, in Exeter Hall and elsewhere, with persuasive and powerful eloquence.

He was the first native ordained preacher in that valley, and it is a singular and pathetic coincidence that the first convert of his ministry was his own mother. His ministry was wonderfully blessed of the Holy Spirit. He preached with great power, was untiring in toil, and saw multitudes brought to Christ. Mission stations were established, the slave trade was arrested and finally destroyed, and the moral and social life of the people almost entirely reconstructed.

In 1864, with solemn and impressive ceremony, he was ordained the first Bishop of the Niger. Thus, under the providence of God, the poor slave boy was made the most distinguished guide and leader of his people into a higher and nobler life.

Shemmas Meekha, of Mosul.

This remarkable man lived on the western coast of Asia, and was born in 1816. In 1828 a plague swept over Mosul, and carried off forty thousand persons. Among the victims was a millwright, the father of Meekha.

The meditative youth early became burdened in spirit, and sought comfort and counsel from the priest of his heathen faith. He studied Syriac, that he might read books and investigate for himself. In the providence of God the Rev. Joseph Mathew, an evangelical graduate of the college at Cattayam, in Southern India, came to Mosul. Meekha soon formed his acquaintance, and for him he had a strong attachment. He was employed as the Arabic teacher of Rev. A. K. Hinsdale, from whom he in turn learned English, and, best of all, a knowledge of the true God.

One Sabbath, while conversing with his teacher

in an "upper room" on redemption through Christ, he drew near, and said eagerly: "Do come with me and repeat these good words to my people, and I will interpret them, for they never heard truth like that." His heart was not only filled with the peace of God, but with an intense concern for the salvation of his people.

While working at the trade of his father he became a teacher and lay preacher, but never felt called to the full functions of a minister. Through his influence largely the truth was so deeply rooted in Mosul that no subsequent persecutions could displace it. He was a Christian of almost perfect consecration. Two of the choice hymns in the Arabic hymn book used by the Syrian Mission were from his pen, and he left an unfinished Syriac manuscript translation of "Pilgrim's Progress."

In writing to a missionary friend he says: "Pray that God will keep me from sloth, and make me perfect in his service. I long to impart to others that knowledge of an atoning Saviour which God has given me. How can I describe the greatness of my obligation for this grace? I grieve to see so many without Christ. Pray that I may have grace to instruct them to believe; and yet, should I bring the whole world to him, that would be the work of his power and grace, not mine."

In another letter he said: "I think I know something of that sweet word of John, '*There is no fear in love;*' and I know that nothing can separate me from his love. I try to lead men to Christ. Some approve my words, but yield no fruit; yet I hope that if the grain of wheat fall into the ground and die it will not remain alone."

He peacefully fell asleep June 14, 1881. So highly was he esteemed and so profoundly revered that the Christians had him buried inside the church, "that they might be constantly reminded of the gospel he taught them while alive."

We have had his own statement of his inner spiritual life; now let us look at his outward conduct, as seen by others. His high Christian character commands not only respect, but admiration. Dr. Marsh, of the Assyrian Mission, said of him: "His mind was clear, with splendid acuteness and strength, and was very receptive of truth. He was a thinker rather than an actor; but by unswerving probity among a dishonest people, Christlike gentleness among violent men, and steadfast loyalty to Christ and truth, he bore testimony for God."

The memory of this saintly man's consistent piety abides as an inspiration.

A Remarkable Experience.

Here is another expression of the Spirit's power in the heart of a recent barbarian, restraining his passion for blood and revenge. Few more unmistakable and remarkable triumphs of grace are recorded in the *memorabilia* of the Christian Church. It comes to us from the South Seas.

When the Rev. Mr. Taylor, a missionary in New Zealand, was about to return to England, some years ago, he held a farewell service, concluding with the communion of the Lord's Supper. When the first communicants were kneeling around the chancel, one man arose suddenly, and in great agitation returned to his seat. After some time he recovered composure, and went again to the altar, and partook of the holy sacrament. When afterwards interrogated by the missionary as to his strange conduct, he made answer as follows: " When I approached the table I did not know beside whom I should have to kneel. Then I suddenly saw that I was beside the man who, some years ago, slew my father and drank his blood, and whom I then swore I would kill the first time that I should see him. Now think what I felt when I suddenly knelt beside him. It came upon me with terrible power, and I could not prevent it, so I went back to my seat. Arrived there, I saw, in the spirit, the upper sanctuary, and seemed to hear a voice: 'Thereby shall all men know that ye are my disciples, if ye have love one to another.' That made a deep impression upon me, and at the same time I thought I saw another sight—a cross and a man nailed thereon—and I heard him say: "Father, forgive them; they know not what they do.' Then I went back to the altar."

NAMAKEI, THE OLD CHIEF OF ANIWA.

The first trophy of Dr. John G. Paton's ministry in the New Hebrides was Namakei, the old chief of Aniwa. In early life he was a cannibal and a great warrior; but under the teaching and preaching of Dr. Paton he at length became an earnest Christian, and for many years was the powerful defender of the great missionary, and aided not a little in the rapid extension of the work. Dr. Paton says: " Slowly but very steadily the light of the gospel broke in upon his soul, and he was ever very eager to communicate to his people all that he had learned."

His last act was to attend a Synod on the neighboring island of Aneityum, and there he passed away to the better land. So enraptured was the old chief with the religious fervor of the meeting, and the reported progress of the work, as one island after another was given in as having been won to Christ, that he cried out: "I am lifting up my head like a tree. I am growing tall with joy!"

When prostrated with what he feared was a fatal illness he sent for Dr. Paton, and said: "Missi, I am near to die. I have asked you to come and say farewell. Tell my daughter, my brother, and my people to go on pleasing Jesus, and I will meet them again in the fair world."

When assisted to a cool place under the shade of a banyan tree, he said again to Dr. Paton: "I am going! O Missi, let me hear your words rising up in prayer, and then my soul will be strong to go." As the great missionary knelt by him, the old saint grasped the hand of his teacher, and, pressing it to his heart, said in a strong, clear tone: "O my Missi, my dear Missi, I go before you, but I will meet you again in the home of Jesus. Farewell!"

With these words he relaxed his loving grasp, and sweetly fell on sleep. So "the first person who ever on that island of love and tears opened his heart to Jesus" entered his Master's joy.

In the Training College at Asyat, Egypt, attended by over four hundred boys and young men, nineteen have joined the Student's Volunteer

Movement. Some who offered themselves for the work gave their reasons for so doing as follows:

Christ commanded us to preach the gospel. As I love him, I must keep his commandments.—*Abadir Ibraheem.*

There are few preachers in my country, while there are multitudes of men who know not the truth.—*Gabra Hanna.*

Our country is not small, and its progress depends upon its Christian young men. Therefore I intend to help train the boys in Christianity, so that later they will work for their fellow-men. The Lord's work is wide and the workers few. Our young men prefer to go to the government offices. Therefore I choose to be a Christian teacher to educate the small boys in their youth, so as to be progressive in their old age.—*Kheelaylah Masrood.*

I feel that I am under responsibility because of the religious knowledge the Lord hath given me. I must not hide the light I have, lest my brothers die in the valley of darkness.—*Isshak Ibraheem.*

He who knows something of God, and does not inform others, is responsible before God.—*Handa Gabroos.*

Now, these several experiences of persons widely separated by race, nationality, civilization, heredity, and environment, yet all testifying substantially and joyfully to the same things, are a conclusive and triumphant vindication of Christianity's claims to be the one universal religion. In the language of the eloquent Bishop Alexander, we may say: "By a homage of such diversity and such extent we recognize a universal Saviour for the universal wants of universal man, the fitting Propitiation for the whole world." Therefore, however slow its progress or formidable the opposition to its advance, missionary success is assured and final redemption a divine certainty.

LECTURE IV.

FRUITS FROM VARIOUS FIELDS.

IV.

FRUITS FROM VARIOUS FIELDS.

ARE Missions a failure? is a question the Church is compelled to answer. There is a demand for results that must be respected. And though this urgent demand may indicate an enfeebled faith—an impatience that will not wait upon the sure and mighty movements of God—yet it cannot be disregarded. Though it may be enough for an enlightened faith that the Church is obediently carrying out the orders of the King of kings, still there ought to be some return from the expenditures of a hundred heroic years.

The purpose of this lecture is to rapidly survey some of the great mission fields, and see what report they have to make to the Lord of the harvest. Of course there are many things wrought by the gospel that cannot be tabulated, and are, indeed, scarcely translatable into human speech. To estimate, for instance, the amount of patient, preparatory work necessary to make the world accessible to Christianity is beyond the power of human reckoning. But mighty results have been wrought that all can understand, which attest the all-conquering power of the Christian religion. To some of these attention will be called.

First, all heathen faiths are losing their hold upon intelligent votaries. Under the silent, persistent influence of the gospel faith in old, effete systems is being undermined, and new aspirations are being enkindled, which are prophetic of yet greater results. There is a divine discontent with doctrines and forms that cease to satisfy. In India there is widespread restlessness of thought, and a spirit of eager inquiry has stirred to the depths the stagnation of centuries. In a Madras paper these lines appeared, as voicing the cry of vast multitudes:

> We are weary of empty creeds,
> Of guides who show no man the way,
> Of worship linked with lust and shame:
> Life is an ill, the sea of births is wide,
> And we are weary—who shall be our guide?

Sir Monier Williams says that education is causing a "great upheaving of old creeds and superstitions throughout India, and the ancient fortress of Hindooism is in this way being gradually undermined. *The educated classes look with contempt on idolatry.*"

The Brahmo Somaj, the Theistic Society of India, said by Max Müller to be "the most momentous movement in this momentous century," is itself an expression of the unrest of the Hindoo mind. Despairing of the old faiths, and not yet quite able to fully accept the Christian faith, there is a pathetic feeling after the truth if haply they may find it. But these Brahmos make no secret of their admiration of the character of Jesus Christ, and it is said that in the home of every member there is a picture of the Man of Galilee. An educated Hindoo, and not a professing Christian, in delivering an eloquent address in Bombay, rang out this question and answer: "What has started our present religious Somajas all over India? Contact with Christian missionaries." He concluded his address with these words: "Of one thing I am convinced: Do what we will, oppose as we may, it is the Christian's Bible that will sooner or later work the regeneration of this land." And Keshub Chunder Sen, the able leader of the Brahmo Somaj, went even farther, and said: "You cannot deny that your hearts have been touched, conquered, and subjugated by a superior force. That power, need I tell you, is Christ. It is Christ who rules British India, and not the British Government."

From Sir Charles Atchison, another distinguished authority, we get this positive opinion: "Educated Hindoo society is honeycombed with unbelief, and the great question of the day in India is: 'What shall take the place of the broken gods?'" The Hon. John W. Foster, a distinguished American statesman and diplomat, on his return from the East, in a recent missionary address, testifies to the same thing in these words: " During our sojourn at Calcutta we saw much of the families of several Hindoo gentlemen of the Brahman and Rajpoot castes, leading lawyers, literary and wealthy people of the city, some of them graduates of Cambridge, England, and the equals in intelligence and culture of any European circles. *They recognized the utter folly and emptiness of their religion as practiced by the masses.*"

Another evidence of the conquering progress of Missions is *the awakened opposition to Christianity*. The days of ridicule have been succeeded by widespread alarm. They feel that the foundations are giving away. Hoary superstitions, the massive structures of weary centuries, are toppling to ruin, and the cracking of falling timbers is heard round the world. With pen and tongue the ablest defenders of these false faiths have enlisted for the final struggle. They are in the " throes of heathen despair," and will not see Christianity win a victory without a bitter contest. But this desperation of hostility is confined largely to the priestly classes. In Japan Buddhist priests have taken to preaching to arrest the sweeping progress of the gospel, and in Kioto a Buddhist theological seminary has been built and equipped for the training of men able to defend their decaying doctrines. But every brick in that building is a voiceless but eloquent tribute to the conquering march of the gospel. The dull, monotonous, unintelligible repetition of certain phrases before a dreary altar by an ignorant priest no longer satisfies the eager, persistent questionings of the people. Priests, therefore, must become public teachers and preachers.

In India a Hindoo Tract Society has been established at Madras for the issuance of publications in defense of Brahmanism and malignant attacks upon Christianity. In the plazas and market places their best orators stand to plead with the multitudes. Not only so, but eloquent Hindoos have felt constrained to come to America and appeal to Christians to cease missionary effort in India, because it is a sad and certain failure. They benevolently urge our people no longer to squander their means on a visionary enterprise and a forlorn hope. But if Christianity is making no progress, why should Vivekananda and others make such piteous appeals to the American public? Why be disturbed about a cause in which there is no hope of success? Dr. Jenkins, of England, for years a missionary in India, not long since uttered these significant words: "Just one century ago, in yonder small meetinghouse in Nottingham, there was a question debated by a little Baptist council: 'How can we get Christianity into India?' There is another question debated now by our enemies here and in India: 'How can we get Christianity out of India?'" But the time of its uprooting and transplanting will never come. It can never be gotten out of India, or any other land, where it is firmly planted. And the better informed natives themselves see the hand-writing on the wall, and have not failed in its interpretation. An appeal from certain Hindoos, sent out to arouse the natives to vigorous and united action against Christianity, contained this significant admission: "Missionaries have cast their nets over our children by teaching them in their schools, and they have already made thousands of Christians, and are continuing to do so. Do you not know that the number of Christians is *increasing*, and the number of Hindoo religionists *decreasing* every day?" It was mere bluster when a Buddhist priest said to a Moravian missionary: "I will tell you what you have done here: you have given Buddhism a resurrection." If so, the graveclothes are still on the corpse, and the pallor of death yet on its cheeks. But really there has been no resurrection. The stone has only been rolled from the door of the sepulcher and revealed the ghastliness of the grave.

But there is no diviner evidence of the power of the gospel than its *transformation of heathen houses into homes.* If, as has been beautifully said, "the first consecrating touch of the incarnation rested upon the family," we should expect to find among the first fruits of the gospel of the Incarnate Son of God in heathen lands a reconstructed and purified family life. This is at once the test of a religion and the condition of its triumph. Unless the home, which is the corner stone of the social state, the palladium of national life, and the stronghold of religion, can be reached and reclaimed, there is no hope of redeeming the nations. I reproduce, with heartiest approval, the noble words of Dr. Fairbairn: "A religion that does not purify the home cannot regenerate the race; one that depraves the home is certain to deprave humanity. Motherhood is to be sacred, if manhood is to be honorable. Spoil the wife of sanctity, and for the man the sanctities of life have perished."

The radiating, saving center of a community is

a Christian home. Hence the vast importance of missionaries establishing, as eloquent object lessons to the heathen, bright, cheerful, happy Christian homes. A distinguished missionary statesman did not overestimate the power of such a silent ministry when he uttered these earnest words: " Into the midst of pagan masses—where society is coagulated rather than organized, where homes are degraded by parental tyranny, marital multiplicity, and female bondage—he brings the heaven of a redeemed family, which is to be the nucleus of a redeemed community."

In heathen countries there are no homes, only houses. The basis of family life is tyrannous and grossly immoral. Prof. Monier Williams says that in no Indian tongue is there " any equivalent for that grand old Saxon monosyllable, *Home*— that little word which is the key to our national greatness." And that judgment is confirmed by the Hindoo philosopher, Keshub Chunder Sen, who remarked that a home in Bengal was " a whited sepulcher! There may be exceptions, but this is the rule. The horrors of the zenana are multiplied tenfold by the misery of the joint family system, and the degradation which domestic ill will produces." That certainly is a remarkable admission from a native, who must have spoken by the authority of thorough knowledge. Chief Justice Miyoshi, of Japan, when on a visit to England some years ago, and residing temporarily in a Christian family, uttered these words: "Here I am forty years of age, and I never knew what *home* was before."

Christian Missions, in reconstructing the family life, have put "the bright crown of queenship upon woman's brow." The drudge and slave has been elevated to her rightful throne. Fetters have been broken from her limbs, and the burdens of a beast have been lifted from her chafed and weary shoulders. Christianity alone puts honor upon womanhood. Bishop Alexander has forcefully said: "From her out of whom Jesus cast seven devils to the Chinese woman converted last year, womanhood confesses: 'Christ first taught us that we were women.'"

Her degradation in all heathen countries is beyond power of description or exaggeration. The old Arabic proverb which says that the threshold of the house weeps forty days when a girl is born is the heathen estimate of womanhood. She has no rights to be respected, no feelings to be regarded, no character to be protected, no honor to be defended, no opinions to be considered, and no mind to be educated. In all non-Christian lands, a hundred years ago, there was scarcely a woman able to read. So degraded was her condition and so fixed in social life, that when Dr. Duff first went to India he said that to educate and elevate woman was as difficult as to "scale a wall five hundred feet high." But that wall has been scaled, for it is now stated that "in the province of Bengal alone a hundred thousand women and girls are under instruction," and all over the empire a change amounting to a social revolution has been wrought. To-day there are native lady graduates of universities in several Oriental countries. And it is said that the very appearance of the women tells whether or not a Christian mission has been established in a community, for it must be that, as Dr. Gordon says, "the gospel gives new hands and new faces," as well as new hearts, to those who accept it. Most interesting is this testimony from the distinguished missionary, Dr. J. Murray Mitchell: "In Southern India, for instance, you can tell whether a village is largely Christianized by the appearance of the women at the well: their dress is more seemly, their look is different. Nearly every Hindoo woman has a careworn, anxious face, as if the battle of life tried her sore. The Christian woman has a far more peaceful expression."

As farther evidence of the remarkable and substantial growth of Missions, I quote another striking statement from the recent missionary address of ex-Secretary John W. Foster: "A few months ago I stood at Beyrout, Syria, by the grave of Pliny Fisk, the first missionary. Within a radius of two miles of that grave are four Christian colleges, seven female seminaries, sixty boys' schools, thirty-two girls' schools, seventeen printing presses, and four large hospitals." Two items in that wonderful sentence, were there no others, indicate the measureless distance between us and the earlier days of Pliny Fisk: "*seven female seminaries, and thirty-two girls' schools.*" What that means to the uplifting of India and the redemption of the Orient those can appreciate who have studied the joint family system, and the iniquities of the zenana.

With the knowledge of Christ comes a desire for the comforts and refinements of Christian civilization. While wise missionaries resist any effort to force upon the East the dress and customs of the West—condemn attempts to Europeanize and denationalize—some changes are necessarily wrought. Modesty is one of the first fruits of Christianity. To Dr. Lindsey we are indebted for this suggestive statement: "Among the Zulus the first sign of approach to Christ is a desire for clothes. A man comes one day and buys a calico shirt; the next day, perhaps, and buys a pair of duck pants; then a three-legged stool, for he can no longer sit on the ground; and with shirt and pants on, and seated on that stool, he is a thousand miles above the level of the heathen around him."

And like testimony is borne by a United States Minister to Turkey. Referring to the influence of American missionaries on the habits of the people, and the work being done by the colleges at Constantinople, Alexandria, Cairo, Asyoot, and Beyrout, he uses this strong language: " The Arab youth who has graduated at the college in Beyrout is no longer contented to live in a mud pen, to clothe himself in filthy rags, or not at all, and to live on sugar cane. He aspires to live as do his teachers, who come from the great republic on the other side of the Atlantic Ocean. He tells his family and friends something of what he has learned; and an ambition, a longing for something better than they have ever known, is inspired in them."

Christianity also *increases the wealth-producing capacity of a people*. It touches the mainspring of enterprise, unlocks latent energies, and gives wise direction to awakened industry. Dr. George

Smith, the historian of modern Missions, makes this statement as to India: "No statistics can show the growth of these native Christians in wealth, in social position, in official and professional influence. They are pushing out the Brahmans, by character, by ability, and by intelligent loyalty, until the Hindoo press confesses the fact with apprehension, and the local blue books report it continually to Parliament." A large proportion of those reached and redeemed by the gospel are of the humbler classes—the poor to whom the Master preached. And on that account Christianity is ridiculed as the religion of coolies and pariahs. But by its uplifting power the poorest are enriched and outcasts are given such dignity and influence until the highest castes are forced to do them reverence. There is a royalty in the blood of Christ that gives rank to a pariah, and improves a hundredfold the earthly estate of a coolie. Missionary annals are crowded with incidents which strikingly illustrate this suggestive fact.

This multiplied power of achievement is also conferred upon nations with their acceptance of the Christian religion. The wealth of the world is in Christian treasuries. The commerce of the world is controlled by Christian countries. The tonnage of the world is carried almost entirely in vessels flying the flags of Christian nations. And it is also suggestive that the tonnage of Protestant countries is nearly six times as great as that of the Roman Catholics. Race and climatic conditions do not account for this vast difference in wealth and dominion. It is the type of a people's religion that determines their earthly as well as their heavenly estates. A new heaven creates a new earth. Christianity has an industrial value beyond possible calculation. No wonder, therefore, that the new Lieutenant Governor of Bengal, speaking as a government official, and noting the influence of the Christian religion upon the citizenship, social condition, and industrial development of the empire, uttered these emphatic words: "I make bold to say that if Missions did not exist it would be our duty to invent them."

The non-Christian natives in all the mission fields are beginning so to appreciate the commercial value of Christianity that they are placing their children in mission schools to be educated. The most popular institutions in China to-day are those conducted by Christian missionaries. And these sentences from the most influential non-Christian newspaper in India, the *Hindu*, show the drift of intelligent native sentiment in that great empire:

The progress of education among the girls of the native Christian community, and the absence of caste restrictions, will eventually give them an advantage which no amount of intellectual precocity can compensate the Brahmans for. We recently printed the statement of a Bombay paper that the social eminence which at the present moment the Parsees so deservedly enjoy was due to these two causes—namely, that their women are educated, and they are bound by no restrictions of caste. These two advantages slowly make themselves felt among our native Christian people, and it is possible that they will soon become the Parsees of Southern India. They will furnish the most distinguished public servants, barristers, merchants, and citizens, among the various classes of the native community.

The tenderness and sympathy introduced by Christianity into heathen countries are one of the striking evidences of its divine power. When it changes the nature it softens the manners and opens a fountain of brotherly sympathy in the heart. Stoicism is converted into pity, savagery into humanity, brutality into brotherhood. Mr. Lecky thus refers to the softening influence of the Christian religion: "As a matter of fact Christianity has done more to quicken the affections of mankind, to promote piety, to create a pure and merciful idea, than any other influence that has ever acted upon the world." And it is said that the charity and help shown by native Christians are in such marked contrast with the hardness and indifference of Mohammedans, Hindoos, and other heathen as to become a convincing appeal for the religion of the Lord Jesus Christ. Some transformations are certainly wonderful, as in the case of Africaner, the first trophy of Moffat's ministry, and thousands of others that might be gathered.

It has also affected the sentiment and life of nations not yet Christian. A spendid illustration comes from Japan and the late Japan-China war. In the ancient capital city of Kioto, Japan, may be seen the famous "Ear Monument," a large mound on which is a stone or marble shaft. Beneath that mound were buried the ears of Coreans killed and captured by the Japanese in a war of the sixteenth century. Such brutality makes one shudder, and to perpetuate it in marble is nothing less than horror. But a change has come over the Sunrise Kingdom. In 1894-95, during the war between Japan and China, the Red Cross Society had charge of all Japanese hospitals, in which sick and wounded Chinese prisoners were cared for as tenderly as the bravest Japanese soldiers. The Empress herself was daily engaged, with her ladies at court, in making bandages and preparing lint, which were used on wounded Chinese and Japanese alike. What a marvelous change! What a vast distance from the "Ear Monument," at Kioto, to the Red Cross hospitals at Hiroshima! And it is a suggestive coincidence that in the city of Kioto, and under the very shadow of that monument to brutality, an orphan asylum for little girls is being established by a native Christian teacher, to which he devotes all his property.

Another most gratifying result has been the development of the *native church* in heathen lands. By this "infant" Church these lands must at last be Christianized. The firm planting of the native church is the ultimate aim of Christian Missions; or, as the distinguished Secretary of the Church Missionary Society says, it is "the development of native churches with a view to their ultimate settlement upon a self-supporting, self-governing, and self-extending system. When this settlement has been effected, the mission will have attained its euthanasia, and the missionary and all missionary agencies can be transferred to the 'regions beyond.'" This ultimate aim in some fields has been already attained, and these vigorous young churches are sending their flaming apostles into other lands. Wise caution should be observed, however, in withdrawing supervision from mission fields.

Dr. Lawrence characterizes the reproductive

spirit of the gospel in these striking words: "*Every church should work out into a mission; every mission should work out into a church.*" The rapidity with which some missions have worked out into self-sustaining and self-extending churches reveal the same supernatural power that attended the successful ministry of St. Paul. Dr. Mackay, who reported 2,546 baptisms in fifteen years, makes this cheering statement: "If the Church in North Formosa were now left without foreigners or foreign help, I believe that it would grow and prosper. The people know enough of the gospel to appreciate it, and at each chapel they would manage to find sufficient to support a preacher, so that he might give himself wholly to the work of preaching and teaching."

An intelligent young Japanese Christian, in a letter written but a few months ago, uttered these confident words: "I thank God that his religion has found such a deep root in Japan that, even if all missionary efforts are withdrawn from my country, Christianity will go on her way just the same."

From the Samoan group of islands, with a Christian population of over thirty thousand souls, comes intelligence that not only thrills our faith, but is a suggestive lesson to the Church at home. Besides supporting their own ministry, a few years ago they sent a thank offering, as their custom is, of £1,800, to the London Missionary Society. When a Church member dies, they still keep his name on the books, with a mark opposite which means: "We cannot think of him as dead, either to us or to the work. We shall give a contribution in his name, that the cause may not suffer by his removal hence." And to the northwest of Samoa there are ten thousand people who have been won from heathenism by Samoans.

From China the missionaries send like hopeful assurance. In large portions of the Shantung and other provinces, churches are almost entirely self-supporting, though the people are distressingly poor. Instances, eloquent and numerous, could be given. Time would fail to tell of a Taoist priest in a country village, soundly converted, and then converting his house into a chapel that he might preach to his neighbors, without salary; of a true-hearted woman, the only Christian in a community, praying and working until she secured a school which grew into a church: of a little Church, on the day of its separate organization, subscribing the entire salary of a pastor—and scores of others that glorify the annals of the Church in China, and are surely recorded in the chronicles of the skies. Dr. Nevins says: "Experience in China shows that now, as in the early history of the Church, Christianity may be speedily and widely propagated by the spontaneous and silent influence of native Christians." There can be no doubt of the sincere faith of those humble Christians in Ceylon, who are giving their labor when needed, and, tithing their poverty for the Lord, *take out a handful of rice from every day's meal* and consecrate it to God. Such self-denial we have not elsewhere found—no, not in Israel. In Uganda, entered a few years since, so rapid and widespread is the enlargement of the work that already one hundred native laborers are in the field, all supported *by native contributions*. The South India Missions, connected with the Church Missionary Society, contributed in one year $13,582 in gold. And from India, Burmah, and Ceylon the aggregate contributions from native Christians rapidly increased from 60,000 rupees in 1861 to 159,124 in 1871, and to 228,517 rupees in 1881. And it is a gratifying fact that by far the larger portion of converts in India are to-day won to Christ by the agency of the native ministry. Bishop Thoburn states that one hundred native teacher-preachers reported 1,400 converts in one year.

Most instructive is the story of the Church of England Mission in Fuchow. In 1862 there were only three converts, and they turned out unsatisfactorily. One missionary died, and the other had to leave for a few months on account of failing health. In his absence a Chinese mob set fire to the mission buildings. So, after twelve years of toil, the whole mission apparently collapsed. But the brave missionary, though advised against it, under the guidance of the Holy Spirit, returned to the ashes of his former labors and began to lay anew the foundation of the kingdom. At the end of 1893 there were 170 places of worship in that province, 11,000 Christian adherents, 125 catechists, and 106 schoolmasters. "These blessed results," said Archdeacon Wolfe, "are, under God, mainly due to the free employment of a native agency which, from 1862 to the present time, has ever been liberally used in this mission."

At Sierra Leone there is a "self-sustaining and self-extending" African Church. The only white clergyman in the colony is Bishop Ingram. All pastoral work is in the hands of native ministers, who are represented as efficient and zealous.

But even more remarkable has been the progress among the Karens of Burmah. After sixty years of labor there are forty thousand communicants in the Church and one hundred thousand adherents, with numerous schools and a foreign missionary society. In 1894 over sixteen thousand rupees were contributed for Church and school purposes. The British Government report some years ago referred to the " four hundred and fifty-one Christian Karen parishes, most of which support their own Church parish school and native pastor, and many of which subscribe considerable sums for missionary work," and added this tribute to their personal character: " These Christian Karen communities are so much more industrious, better educated, and more law-abiding that the British Government owes a vast debt to the American missionaries under whom this change has been wrought." The late and long-to-be-lamented Dr. Gordon said that, though only fifty years out of heathenism, " the poor Karens of Burmah outrank their Baptist brethren of every State in the American Union save two as contributors to their missionary society."

The Fijians, but a few years ago the worst of cannibals, are now the most active and heroic missionaries. They enterprised the work in New Britain, New Ireland, and other neighboring islands themselves, and in the prosecution of the same have cheerfully suffered persecutions for their Lord that deserve large place in the chronicles of Christian martyrdom.

The transforming power of the Holy Spirit seems even more wonderful when we look at *the character of these native Christians*. Amiel says that " the test of every religious, political, or educational system is the man which it forms." By that test the fruit of Missions can stand. They are not mere " paper converts," as has been sneeringly charged—good only to count and deceive the Church at home—but display the same genuine marks of the Christ life as may be seen in England or the United States. The British Governor, Sir Arthur Gordon, reporting to his government, paid this tribute to the Fijians: " Out of a population of about one hundred and twenty thousand *one hundred and two thousand* are now regular worshipers in the churches, which number eight hundred, all well built and completed. *In every family there is morning and evening worship.*" Such a percentage of Church attendance and such attention to family religion can scarcely be paralleled in all the world. In the largest of the Samoan Islands it is said that there " cannot be found fifty families that fail to observe family worship," and of the spiritual character of the work there the *Herald of Missions* says: " We don't know if the tide of devotion has reached as high a watermark anywhere else the wide world over."

After the missionaries had been forty years in the Hawaiian Islands they were visited by the Hon. Richard H. Dana, who, in writing of his observations, made this interesting statement: "I did not find a hut without a Bible and hymn book, and family worship and grace at meals are as universal as they were a hundred years ago in New England." And ten years later those islands were visited by Mr. Moncure D. Conway, an apostle of liberal thought. He was disappointed almost to disgust. Instead of witnessing, as he expected and said, "merry scenes, islanders swimming around the ship in Arcadian innocence, and the joyous dance and song of the guileless children of the sun," he saw in Honolulu a "silent city, paralyzed by piety," and said that he had to "go to church to see people." "Never in Scotland or Connecticut," said he, "have I seen such a paralysis as fell upon Honolulu the first day of the week." It was not the purpose of this boasted apostle of culture to make an admission in favor of Christianity, but such is the eloquent prelude and interlude of every word that he has written. Would to God that a like "paralysis of piety" could characterize the Sabbath of ours and every land!

A distinguished Hollander, who visited Sumatra

and made an extensive tour through the Dutch East Indies, and who before his travels had an unconcealed prejudice against Missions, has made this statement: "To be welcomed in the land of cannibals by children singing hymns, this, indeed, shows the peace-creating power of the gospel." James Chalmers, of New Guinea, gives a graphic account of a Christmas sacramental service in his mission, in which he says: "I was united with, and shed tears of joy with, men and women who a few years before sought our lives. What did it? It is the old story still of the gospel of Christ."

Carl Ritter, who has been called the "prince of geographers," said that the transformation in the character of the natives of New Zealand is "the standing miracle of the age." Of these New Zealanders Bishop Selwyn, with a larger knowledge of the field, also wrote: "We see here a whole nation of pagans converted to the faith. Where will you find throughout the Christian world more signal manifestations of the presence of the Spirit, or more living evidences of the kingdom of Christ?"

The Chinese Christians compare favorably with any other race in the strength of their faith, the solidity of their character, and the genuineness of their Christian experience. Many testimonies could be given. This from a discriminative student of the mission fields of the world, the late Fleming Stevenson, is very clear: "I have found nowhere in Christian lands men and women of a higher type than I met in China, of a finer spiritual experience, of a higher spiritual tone, or a nobler spiritual life, and I may say with conviction that there are in the native churches in China not only the elements of stability, but that steadfast and irresistible revolution which will carry over the whole empire to the new faith." It was a Chinese Christian, Lough Fook, who sold himself into slavery and shipped to the South American mines, that he might have readier spiritual access to his countrymen. And he had the joy, before his translation, of seeing nearly two hundred of them converted to God, and devout members of a Christian Church. Of this beautiful instance of lowly consecration—taking upon himself the form of a slave—Dr. Gordon says: "To a Christian Chinaman belongs, so far as we know, the unique honor of wearing the Saviour's bonds in voluntary servitude."

During the recent massacres in Armenia, which awoke universal horror and indignation, atrocities have been committed almost without a parallel in the past century. And on the other hand there have been examples of triumphant faith and heroic endurance among native Christians, worthy of conspicuous mention in the later acts of the apostles. At least twenty native pastors have suffered death rather than deny their Lord, while hundreds of other Christians have filled martyrs' graves. Writing under date of February 27, 1896, a missionary tells this thrilling story: " During the massacre at Ourfa two young men were seized by the mob. They were asked to accept Islamism, and were told that refusal was death. The mother of the young men stood by, and said to them: ' Die, but do not deny the Lord Jesus.' They stood firm, and were immediately cut down by the cruel swords of the Moslems." When Bishop Hannington went down to his glorious martyrdom in Uganda, he was accompanied by *thirty-two native Christians*, " massacred in one lot," whose dying testimony was not only triumphant, but even jubilant.

Nor less emphatic and genuine is the testimony of some tourists and scholars to the transforming power of the Christian religion. Conspicuous among these is the name of Charles Darwin, the great naturalist, and not supposed to be in active sympathy with the Christian Church and its missionary enterprises. But these are his words, and a severe rebuke they are to shallow critics of Foreign Missions:

> They forget, or will not remember, that human sacrifice and the power of an idolatrous priesthood; a system of profligacy unparalleled in any other part of the world; infanticide, a consequence of that system; bloody wars, where the conquerors spared neither women nor children—that all these things have been abolished, and that dishonesty, intemperance, and licentiousness have been greatly reduced by the introduction of Christianity. In a voyager to forget these things is a base ingratitude; for should he chance to be at the point of shipwreck on some unknown coast, he will most devoutly pray that the lesson of the missionary may have extended thus far.

Alfred Russell Wallace, the scientist, who wrote a charming volume on the Malay Archipelago, thus speaks of the mighty achievements of the missionaries in those islands, where he spent so much time in the study of man and nature: "The missionaries have much to be proud of in this country. They have assisted the government in changing a savage into a civilized community in a wonderfully short space of time. Forty years ago the country was a wilderness, the people naked savages, garnishing their rude houses with human heads. Now it is a garden worthy of its sweet native name of 'Minahati.'"

Capt. Briggs, in his interesting book, "Sunny Days in Salween," makes this generous statement:

"As an official of eight or nine years' experience on this coast, I can vouch for the great moral elevation among the Christian Karens. I venture to assert that ten Christian villages give less trouble to the police than one heathen Karen village. Indeed, our registers show that in one heathen town, Taung by uk, there is more crime than in the whole Christian district of this province."

The speedy development of ethical life in those so recently emancipated from the bondage of heathen superstition is pathetically illustrated in the first letter written in English by a Congo native, and for which I am indebted to Dr. Pierson. It is addressed to the Archbishop of Canterbury:

> Great and Good Chief of the tribe of Christ; Greeting: The humblest of your servants kisses the hem of your garment, and begs you to send to his fellow-servants more gospel and less rum. In the bonds of Christ. UGALLA.

And we are made to rejoice over the *rapid progress of Missions*. The movement has been accelerated far beyond the faith of the Church. The harvest is large, the results marvelous. When we consider the resources at command, the opposition that had to be encountered, the barriers to be broken down, and the almost insurmountable difficulties to be overcome, we cannot but be amazed at the majestic movement of the missionary cause. The vastness of its achievements can only be accounted for by a recognition of the constant presence and assistance of a supernatural power. And yet objection is heard that Missions make slow progress. In this demand for rapid results there may be evidence of an enfeebled faith, a desire to walk by sight. That is the sturdiest and truest confidence in God that laboriously works, and then cheerfully waits. We are too "idolatrous of the immediate." To this objection Archbishop Whateley once made reply as follows: "The man that is in a hurry to see the full effects of his tillage must cultivate annuals, and not forest trees." Our Lord waited long for "the fullness of time;" and as we are building for the eternities, we can well afford to spend ample time on the foundations.

But progress has not been slow. The angel of the apocalypse has flown on swift wing. Nations have been born almost in a day. And this progress, which has been a perpetual miracle, must increase in ratio; for each convert is not a dead figure to count, but a living influence to work. So the ratio of growth must continually increase. It is geometrical. Max Müller well says: "An intellectual harvest must not be calculated by adding simply grain to grain, but by counting each grain

FRUITS FROM VARIOUS FIELDS. 147

as a living seed, that will bring forth fruit a hundred and a thousand fold."

It was failure to consider this vital fact that led Canon Taylor into fatal error. His arithmetic would never have told so lugubrious a tale and his disparagements of missionary activity and results would not have been so contemptuous, had he not mistaken living souls for dead figures. Comparing the birth rate in heathen lands with the number of conversions in all mission fields for a series of years, and assuming that the same ratio would continue—that the present rate of increase will be the perpetual rate—he employed the scornful figure of the tortoise and the train to travesty the utter weakness and humiliating failure of modern Missions. But the ratio of increase is not stationary. Movement in some fields has been by leaps and bounds, while in almost every other the progression has been geometrical. The tortoise has overtaken the train.

Protestant mission work began in Madagascar, "the Great Britain of Africa," in 1818. The fruit of ten years' labor was only fifty native catechumens. Then came the days of bitter persecution which drove the missionaries from the field. Yet in 1868 there were 37,112 Christians, and in 1878, just ten years later, *there were 250,000.* In Japan, after nearly twenty years of preparatory work, there were 3,000 Christians in 1876; this number increased to 14,500 in 1882, and in five years more to 43,000. But even more suggestive are the last figures from another field, and a single mission. Dr. E. W. Parker, of the Methodist Episcopal Mission in India, said that in 1891 their converts were increasing at the rate of 6,000 per year. In 1893 Bishop Thoburn said that the rate had advanced to nearly fifty a day, or about 17,000 per year; and in 1894 the increase was *thirty thousand*. Indeed, the remarkable success of that and other missions in India has occasioned the most serious problem of the hour—has precipitated a veritable crises in opportunity and administration.

With the marvelous transformation in Fiji the world is now familiar. What a change in only forty years! Cannibal islands become thoroughly Christian—churches built on " the site of cannibal ovens "—and out of a population of 110,000, 104,000 regularly and reverently attending places of public worship. James Calvert said: " When I arrived at the Fiji group, my first duty was to bury the hands, feet, heads, and bones of arms and legs of eighty victims whose bodies had been roasted and eaten in a cannibal feast. I lived to see the *very cannibals* who had taken part in that inhuman festival gathered about the Lord's table."

What a history of apostolic achievement is contained in that two-line inscription to Dr. John Geddie, in the Church at Aneityum:

WHEN HE LANDED HERE IN 1848 THERE WERE NO CHRISTIANS;
WHEN HE LEFT HERE IN 1872 THERE WERE NO HEATHEN.

Reports like this from many of the great harvest fields, made by Dr. Mansell, are now by no means exceptional: "In 1890 Dr. Wilson, of Budayoon, in only eleven months baptized 1,163; Dr. Buchner, of Bijiore, baptized 533; Hazan Raza Kahn, of Kas Ganj, baptized 415; Ibrahim Solomon, a converted Jew, of Farthgaj, baptized 477. In 1889 there had been 4,000 baptisms; in 1890 there were nearly 9,000; and in 1891 there have been about 18,000, while only in a small part of the field 20,000 more are reported as ready for membership in the Church."

After years of self-denying toil and patient waiting, the Moravian missionaries in the far-away, frozen parallels of Labrador witnessed a Pentecost. It is said that "the churches could not contain the numbers who flocked to hear the message of salvation," and soon the whole land was traversed by native evangelists, baptized by the Holy Ghost, and preaching with persuasive power. Dr.

Pierson tells us of a single missionary station in the East, near the Bosporus, which in fourteen years established a central nucleus, with twelve out stations, and seven of them containing self-supporting Christian churches. "All that work of fourteen years," he says, "was accomplished with less money than built the church in the city of Detroit in which I preached for thirteen years."

So rapid indeed has been the march of Christianity, and so extensive its conquests, that we may say almost of the entire world, as Tertullian did of Christian evangelism in the country he knew: "We are but of yesterday, and we have filled all that belongs to you—the cities, the fortresses, the free towns, the very camps, the palace, the senate, the forum; we leave to you the temples only." And in most heathen countries the old, decayed temples are sadly neglected, and scarcely a new one is being erected.

And these magnificent results have been wrought with seemingly insufficient means. There is no correspondence between the means employed and the ends achieved. The fact that obscure fishermen, unlettered, and without official influence, and in the face of fierce fanaticism and political prejudice, wrought the mighty results they did, evidenced beyond question the presence and power of

God. So we are forced to a like explanation of the marvelous transformations in the mission field. They were not an evolution, but a spiritual revolution. Consecrated men, clothed only with a power from on high,

> Mitered with pentecostal flame

by the simple truths they declared, have changed the map of the world.

And this rapid progress is the more suggestive when we study the comparative success of the home and foreign work. Last year it was estimated that, while there were about *seven converts* to each of the preachers of the United States, there were *seventy converts* to each of the missionaries in Asia. *Seven and seventy*. With an equal number of laborers the harvest is ten times greater in the regions beyond. And yet some object to Foreign Missions because of their meager results. In the Presbytery of Shantung, in Northern China, in 1891, 760 persons were admitted to the communion of the Church. There were only nine Presbyteries in the United States, including the great centers of influence and population, that made a like report. And ex-Secretary of State, John W. Foster, in a missionary address, said a few weeks ago that "the statistics for the Presbyterian Church last year show that the ratio of additions to the native churches in India alone was nearly twice as great as in the churches in America."

The following admirable and gratifying summary of results in India, by Rev. J. E. Scott, is only a sample of the fruits in almost every mission field:

1. Caste is breaking down. It is seen in the way people eat and drink, dress and work; in the way they travel, in their schools, on their trains, steamships, and in their mills.

2. The poor are coming up. The coming man in India is the converted sweeper.

3. The people are broadening out. The National Congress, the Social Congress, the newspapers, the patronage of Western science, the study of law, medicine, and engineering—all indicate that.

4. Christ is honored more. Many among all classes now look upon him with favor. Brahmos, Brahmans, and Mohammedans speak well of him.

5. The Christian Missions are succeeding. Never before in the history of India were they advancing so rapidly as now. "The workers were never so numerous, the schools never so spiritual, the methods never so good, the fraternity and unity never so strong, the converts never so numerous, the Church never so spiritual as now."

6. The native Church is taking hold. Often it is becoming self-supporting. The people are appreciating their own pastors. Strong men are being raised up.

7. All feel it worth the effort. Here are 282,000,000 people.

Looking at these stupendous achievements of the gospel in overturning the false faiths of the world and establishing a kingdom "wherein dwelleth righteousness," I most heartily adopt the eloquent words of Dr. Storrs, as applied to an earlier period: "It conquered, where philosophies had failed; it exalted, where arts had degraded; it purified, where religions had polluted; and, in the eloquent words of another, 'it made the instrument of the slave's agony a symbol more glorious than the laticlave of consuls or the diadem of kings.' The splendor of that supreme achievement no skepticism can shadow, no lapse of time rob of its brightness."

But I need not multiply witnesses and add to this splendid volume of inspiring testimony. So abundant and eloquent are these facts—all attesting the same thing, unmistakably asserting their connection with the same divine source and influence—that to deny the divinity of their origin would require a greater strain upon our faith and reason to account for them in some other way. It has been well said: "If Christianity be not of God, then is it historically and structurally a series of miracles unique in the world's history, a miracle greater than its assumed supernaturalism itself."

LECTURE V.

THE MESSAGE OF MISSIONS TO THE CHURCH.

V.

THE MESSAGE OF MISSIONS TO THE CHURCH.

WHEN the disciples of the imprisoned and despondent John the Baptist were dispatched to Jesus, with the strange message, "Art thou he that should come, or do we look for another?" his only response was the display of his miracle-working power. With a seeming indifference to their urgent, distressful request, he continued his mighty works—healing the sick, cleansing the leper, raising the dead, preaching to the poor—and after a time quietly turned to the messengers and said: "Go back and tell John what you have seen and heard." As much as to say: "That will answer his doubts and cheer his fainting faith." In the works that only God can perform he will see the Divine, the One "that should come," and will never again "look for another."

A like response our Lord makes from all the fields where, by his command, missionaries have gone to disciple the nations, and where his miracles of grace are being daily and mightily wrought. He simply says: "Go back and tell the Church what you have seen and heard—how that the blind see, the lame walk, the lepers are cleansed, the dead are raised, and the poor have the gospel preached unto them." Thus God is "*bearing witness*, both with signs and wonders, and with divers miracles, and gifts of the Holy Ghost, according to his will." By the stupendous success of his word, under his own personal administration and the power of the Holy Ghost, he furnishes the infallible proofs of his divinity, and the gospel's perfect adaptation to all nations, and its entire availability for all circumstances, for all races, and for all times.

The purpose of this lecture is to interpret the message of those miracles to the Church. For, as St. Augustine has well said, "our Lord worked miracles to signify somewhat by those miracles, and that we should learn something more from them than simply that they were great, wonderful, and divine." We are to discover, if possible, the "somewhat" signified by the miracles of Missions in all the fields; what lessons they have to teach the Church, while blessing and redeeming the lost millions of heathen lands. And I doubt not it will be ascertained that while they are uplifting the nations abroad, there is a corresponding edification of the Church at home. Thus the mission fields become the most thoroughly furnished and effective teacher at whose feet the Church can humbly sit and eagerly learn. A distinguished German writer has said: " No *doctrine* can bring it about that there shall arise in our hearts the full certainty that God exists for us; only a fact can inspire such confidence in us. Our certainty of God has its root in the fact that within the realm of history to which we ourselves belong we encounter the man Jesus as an undoubted reality."

Missions have made the world known. They have colored the maps of geographers, have traced the lines of nations and empires, have revealed the racial and tribal peculiarities of unknown peoples, and really furnished most of the materials upon which philosophy speculates and commerce plans its gigantic enterprises.

Missions have increased the Church's knowledge of the world's needs. They have uncovered its woes, and articulated its cry for help. Much of the intense opposition which William Carey encountered, and the bitter raillery he endured, were born of ignorance of heathen peoples. Indeed, pagan virtues were applauded. Some men said: " We believe that a Hindoo is milder and soberer than most Europeans, and as honest and chaste." But that time of ignorance has passed away, thanks to the heroic and self-denying toils of Christian missionaries.

Amiel, in his journal, says: "Action coarsens thought." I should rather say that action tests and defines thought. It measures and determines the force of any doctrine. Thus every truth is put to final test. Modern Missions have contributed something, therefore, toward the verification of the great doctrines of the gospel. Prof. Austin Phelps says: " The most triumphant way of proving any doctrine involved in human duty is to use it. Make it thus prove itself as a fact, and time will take care of it as a dogma." We believe that Jesus Christ intended the gospel for all men, and that it is adapted to all men and necessary to all men. We so interpret his great commission, his tasting " death for every man," and his becoming the Propitiation " for the sins of the whole world." These inspired statements we may steadfastly believe. But when we know of different races of men in the various mission fields of the world intelligently apprehending the gospel, attesting its redeeming virtue and illustrating its transforming power, steadfast faith becomes triumphant assurance; and, as Bishop Westcott says, " in the growing assurance that the gospel meets each real need of humanity we shall find the highest conceivable proof of its final and absolute truth." And when the mission fields further testify that no other religion except Christianity " is doing at this time *any regenerating work whatever* for the world "—that all non-Christian faiths are tending to decay—there is left no room for decent doubt.

Among the peoples of earth where mission work has been enterprised there has been found no single exception to the perfect adaptability of the gospel to their real and urgent needs. Charles Kingsley thought that he had discovered one. Taking the position that man might fall by original sin too low for the gospel of Jesus Christ to redeem him, he refers for illustration to the poor Papuan of Australia. He says: " The black people of Australia, exactly the same race as the African negro, cannot take in the gospel. . . . All attempts to bring him to a knowledge of the true God have as yet failed utterly. . . . Poor brutes in human shape, . . . they must perish off the face of the earth like brute beasts." But later reports disprove that statement.

Efforts to reach and reclaim those debased people were most discouraging, traceable, however, to explainable reasons, not creditable to a great Christian nation. But the labors of missionaries have not been entirely fruitless, as the reports of

Moravians abundantly attest. The history of some conversions, and the subsequent life of the believers, evidence that the Holy Spirit can work in their hearts and produce like fruits to those seen among other people.

Missions have given the Church *a broader conception of the great plan of redemption*. It is a curious fact that the doctrine of the divine obligation to give *the world* the gospel has had to win its way in the Church by conquest. Geographical and national prejudices have put limitations upon the scope of our religion. Political and racial antipathies, imported into religious faith, have obscured its divine imperatives and circumscribed the extent of its mission. All religions have been more or less provincial. Some are avowedly and distinctively national. Christianity has not escaped the narrowing influences of political and racial prejudices. They have fettered its spirit, and stayed the majestic march of its world-wide mission of redemption. In the early days of the Church God not only called prophet and apostle wtth his own clear and authoritative voice, but had to employ miraculous agencies to broaden their conceptions and inspire their sense of obligation.

In his Bampton Lectures on " Prophecy a Preparation for Christ " Dr. R. Payne Smith aptly illustrates that thought in this suggestive paragraph on Jonah:

> Now the prophecies generally have a message for the heathen nations round; only two or three confine themselves to Israel and Judah. The heathen nations do not lie beyond the pale of God's providence; and thus Nahum's one subject is Nineveh, Habakkuk's is Chaldea, Obadiah's is Edom. But this is no case merely of sending them a warning, or recording a condemnation of their sins. Jonah has to labor in person among these heathen, and his whole Jewish nature rises up against such a service. He will flee to the ends of the earth rather than *so violate his prejudices.* His name, Jonah, means a "dove;" but he cannot brook the thought of carrying the olive branch to those hateful Assyrians. Nothing short of evident necessity can induce him to obey God's command. So it was with the apostles. Simon Bar-jonah will go and receive the Roman centurion, Cornelius, into the Church only after he has thrice had a command from heaven not to call, in his Jewish way, that common and unclean which the Holy Ghost had sanctified.

And that history has had to be repeated in the Church from the days of Jonah until now. What is known as missionary eras have only been distinguishing points when this sense of obligation was rekindled.

Regeneration, as a great, world-wide enterprise, though not a modern conception, is a distinct modern inspiration. And this inspiration has deepened and strengthened with the majestic advance of missionary forces in heathen lands. For some years after the opening of this last and most brilliant missionary century of the world, the prevailing missionary sentiment was that a few might be restored, but there was no strong faith in the nation's being redeemed. That was only the dream of enthusiasts and visionaries. In 1796, when the subject of Foreign Missions was introduced into the Scottish General Assembly, the proposal was considered preposterous, and vehemently characterized as both "absurd and revolutionary." But now as these triumphs multiply with marvelous rapidity—as nations are sometimes born in a day—we have increasing assurance of the indestructible and conquering vitality of the gospel. We have learned the deeper meaning of those oft-quoted words, "Not by might, nor by power, but by my Spirit, saith the Lord of hosts." Missions have proved to be "a new discovery of divine resources."

And so thought and wrote the calm and cautious Prof. Christlieb of Bonn, in these suggestive words: "The work of Missions is outwardly, at least, more extended than it ever was before. In this region, therefore, according to our former rule, miracles should not be entirely wanting. Nor are they. We cannot, therefore, fully admit the proposition that no more miracles are performed in our day. In the history of modern Missions we find many wonderful occurrences *which unmistakably remind us of the apostolic age.*"

The continued and continuing achievements of the gospel in mission fields strengthen faith in its power to save the world. Faith increases with cumulative evidence. Every conversion is another remove from the apologetic period. Salvation is not an experiment. Deliverance is not a vague and uncertain hope. Redemption is not a mere promise. It is a glorious fact attested by the inspiring history of the ages. It is a joyous verity to which millions are bearing blessed testimony. Our Lord is " mighty to save." On his own shoulders he has laid the weight of the world's woe, and by his own divine arm he has undertaken the world's redemption. His power has been tested. And by these signs and wonders the Church has been led to expect greater things from God, and to attempt greater things for God.

And this strengthened faith in the gospel has increased the Church's sense of indebtedness to the Christless millions, and led to enlarged plans for their redemption. Without faith in the possible salvation of all men there can be no adequate effort for the recovery of all men. We must believe in the perfect adaptation of the gospel to all men, its adequate provision *for* all men, and its final extension to all men.

The Church has been led to believe that the conversion of the world is *possible and practicable*.

And with this increasing sense of indebtedness come new discoveries of divine resources. We understand somewhat the meaning of the prayer, "Thy kingdom come." It is not that independently God will usher in his kingdom, but these words are an appeal and a pledge. "I will do all I can to make thy kingdom come."

Modern Missions have contributed to a clearer estimate of the priceless value, and stronger faith in the mighty power, of God's Word. Translated into the various languages and dialects of the world, testimonies to its enlightening and redeeming sufficiency have multiplied a thousandfold. Each translation has been a signal providence, and the history of some editions has been a miracle. We are thus better able to understand that strange, ominous statement: that the Lord is "jealous of his Word above all his name." The most sacred thing to him in all this world is his Word. If men trifle with his name—with his perfections and powers—they must not tamper with his Word.

Paul's greatest boast was not that he had fought

a good fight—met and mastered the last enemy—not that he had finished his course—triumphantly reached the end of an honored and useful career; but that he had *kept the faith*. He had preserved and preached it in its integrity and entirety, in its purity and power. Without admixture of human tradition, without accommodation to the world's wisdom, without weakening its divine imperatives, without lowering its high standards, he had kept the faith—the whole faith. He called the Ephesian elders to witness, and with pardonable pride, that he had not shunned to declare the *whole counsel of God*.

Now Paul would not have boasted of having kept the faith if it were not worth keeping. His vision had too wide a sweep—he had too ample and accurate a knowledge of the world and its needs—to spend thought and labor on preserving anything of minor importance. With his marvelous power of discrimination he never would have placed such sacred emphasis upon a matter of secondary concern. But he knew that it was the basis of character, the foundation of hope and salvation, the inspiration of spiritual achievement.

" The words that I speak unto you they are spirit and they are life," is the declaration of our Lord himself. The splendid achievements of the mission fields were impossible without the Bible translated into the vernacular of the nations. For, as Dr. Gordon has said, in a sentence as lucid as luminous: "Without the Scriptures Christianity may be *imposed upon* a nation, but it cannot be *implanted in* a nation." And this implanting is the absolute condition of a nation's regeneration.

A striking confirmation of this fact comes from Uganda. Bishop Hirsh, chief of the Roman Catholic Missions, in a report of his vast diocese, makes this suggestive statement: "I am compelled to acknowledge that we will be forced to print a translation of the New Testament, which is being spread by the Protestants all over the country. We cannot *prevent* our people from reading it, for every one, with the women and aged people, wishes to learn to read before being baptized. We are, therefore, busy with an edition of the New Testament, with commentaries by the Fathers of the Church."

This yielding, though under the compulsion of necessity, is a long step forward, especially when considered in connection with other well authenticated facts of history.

The King of Bohemia on one occasion entreated the pope that the Church service might be performed in the language of the country, to which the holy father thus replied: "Dear son, know that we can by no means grant your request; for, having frequently searched the Holy Scriptures, we have discovered that it hath pleased and still pleases Almighty God to direct his worship to be conducted in a hidden language. . . . Therefore, what your people ignorantly require can in no wise be conceded to them, and we now forbid by the power of God and his holy apostle Peter."

The two divinely appointed agencies for the saving of the nations are "the man of God, the Christian preacher; and the Word of God, the Christian Scriptures." These two must go together. But there have been instances, when the "man of God" was lacking, that the "Word of God" alone wrought its redeeming work. This is strikingly illustrated in the strange story of the Pitcairn Islanders. Not by means of a consecrated evangelist, but by the power of the word in the hands of the wicked mutineer, John Adams, those islands are won from superstition and cannibalism to the Lord Christ. From the wreck of a vessel a Bible and prayer book were rescued. Having nothing else to read, these two books were used to while away the tedium of the days. But the Holy Spirit sealed the word to his joyous salvation. He was converted, became a missionary, and witnessed the mighty works of God. So as a distinguished missionary writer says: "One stray copy of the blessed Book of God, and a book of common prayer, in the hands of a reckless, godless mutineer, first became blessing and salvation to himself, and then to that degraded class by whom he was surrounded."

When Dr. William Goodell completed his translation of the Bible into Armenio-Turkish in 1841, he said: "Thus have I been permitted by the goodness of God to dig a well in this distant land, at which millions may drink." And a like enthusiasm of hope stirred the heart of Robert Moffat to rapture on finishing the translation of the Bible into the language of the Bechuanas. He thus graphically relates his experience: "I felt it to be an awful thing to translate the Book of God. When I had finished the last verse, I could hardly believe that I was in the world, so difficult was it for me to realize that my work for so many years was completed. A feeling came over me as if I should die. My heart beat like the strokes of a hammer. My emotions found vent by falling on my knees and thanking God for his grace and goodness in giving me strength to accomplish my task." And the great heart of the sturdy Scotchman, John G. Paton, became even more fervent at the thought of giving the South Sea Islanders God's blessed Word in their own tongue. To any but the ear of faith, and one acquainted with the mysterious and resistless power of the Word, the conduct of the noble missionary, in striking off the first page of his translation into the Tamil language, seems the extravagance of an enthusiast. He says: " Do you think me foolish when I confess that I shouted in an ecstasy of joy when the first sheet came from the press all correct? It was about one o'clock in the morning. I was the only white man then on the island, and all the natives had been fast asleep for hours. Yet I literally pitched my hat into the air, and danced like a schoolboy round and round that printing press, till I began to think, 'I am losing my reason.' Would it be liken a missionary to be upon my knees, adoring God for the first portion of his blessed Word ever printed in this new language? Friends, bear with me: that was as true worship as was even David's dancing before the ark of God."

And a no less intelligent and earnest tribute to the power of the Word comes from the Hawaiian Islands. On the occasion of the formal withdrawal of the American Board of Missions from the field, turning over the administration of the self-sustaining Church to native pastors, whose contributions that year amounted to $30,000, the venerable native missionary, Kanwealola, before a great congregation including the royal family, with a copy of the Bible in the Hawaiian language in hand, uttered these eloquent words: "Not with powder and ball, and swords and cannon, but with this living Word of God, and his Spirit, do we go forth to conquer the islands for Christ."

When the translation of the New Testament was ready for Uganda, it was joyfully seized by the expectant natives. A missionary thus writes: "Talk about sieges, if ever there was a siege, it was yesterday; and this morning it seems likely to be renewed tenfold. I mentioned that our canoe had come, and I gave out on Sunday that the Gospel of St. Matthew would be sold Monday morning. I was roused up before it was light by the roar of voices, and, after dressing hurriedly, sallied out to see—I had almost said fight. Close to my house is a slight shed, used for cows to stand in in the heat of the day. This we barricaded, keeping the people outside; but barricades were useless. In came the door, and we thought the whole place would have fallen. In ten minutes all the hundred Gospels were sold." Bishop Tucker reports the desire for the Scriptures so great that they had to offer an entire invoice for sale at several designated places simultaneously.

And what thrilling personal testimonies to the power of this word come from mission fields! A marvelous history it would make if the various texts that were used by the Holy Spirit in the conversion of the heathen could be collected. It was the story of the Saviour's agony in the garden, that fell into the heart of a stolid savage named Kajarnack, which won the first Christian convert in Greenland; or, as Dr. Gordon poetically says, he is " the first bloom of the rose of Sharon appearing in the frozen field of Greenland."

By such testimonies the faith of the Church is strengthened in the power of the word to redeem all men, and the whole of man.

Another message of Missions to the Church is this: *Civilization is impossible without Christianization.* It is the gospel that civilizes and humanizes. The statue of David Livingstone, at Edinburgh, is an heroic figure of the great missionary explorer standing with a Bible in one hand, while the other rests upon an ax. That is a magnificent conception of the true genius of Christianity, and the three agencies of its final triumph: a man, the Bible, and an industrial implement. But an industrial implement in an unskilled hand, a hand untrained by the "man of God" and the "Word of God," will never pioneer or plant civilization in any land. Dr. Storrs only echoes the "answering voice of history" when he says: "No religion save that of the New Testament can put the moral basis beneath human society and human civilization." Every attempt to civilize without the gospel has proved a disastrous failure. Yet these failures and follies are repeated. And there are some who, as Dr. Gordon says, while they "believe that the Word of God is the 'sword of the Spirit,' are yet tempted to believe that that sword needs civilization as the hilt for grasping it and driving it home."

Samuel Marsden, the pioneer of New Zealand, in his early missionary career, said that "civilization must work in preparation for conversion." After twenty years he wrote down this very different but more mature judgment: "Civilization is not necessary before Christianity. We may give them both simultaneously, if we will; but it will always be found that civilization follows Christianity, rather than conversely. If we speak with the poor heathen of his God and the Saviour, he will understand. The rest will come of itself." But concrete examples are more convincing than the clearest statements or strongest opinions of most trustworthy witnesses. I recall, therefore, the experimental test made by Bishop Colenso in Africa. He selected twelve Zulu lads and took them into his service, using every possible art and influence upon them, except the gospel. Christian teaching was rigidly excluded. When the time expired, every one returned to barbarism, leaving his European clothes behind him. The next day, it is said, the good Bishop went over to the American Mission, and left a note for fifty pounds, with this statement: "You were right, and I was wrong." And even more suggestive is the story told of Hongi, the New Zealand chief, who spent some time in London, and was thought to be quite civilized. But on his return to New Zealand, and engaging in a tribal war, it is related that "the first thing he did, after a battle in which he was victorious, was to tear out and swallow the right eye of his slain enemy, and to bite into his fluttering heart, while he served hundreds of his foes as food for his victorious army."

James Calvert, whose life was spent among the Fijians, and who saw those people rise from the degradation of cannibalism to a stage of civilization that has commanded the attention of the world, made this strong statement: "I have never talked with a single man or woman, or with a single people, that your civilization without Christianity has civilized. Wherever there has been the slightest spark of civilization in the South Seas, it has been where the gospel has been preached. Civilization! The rampart can only be stormed by those who carry the *cross*."

These, and other testimonies that might be gathered into a ponderous volume of evidences, all confirm the statement of the great historian, Mr. James A. Froude, who said: "All that we call modern civilization in a sense which deserves the name is the visible expression of the transforming power of the gospel."

Mr. Huxley gives expression to a despairing sentiment, in contemplating the outlook of society, when he declared that "if there is no hope of a large improvement of the condition of the greater part of the human family . . . I would hail the advent of some kindly comet which should sweep the whole affair away, as a desirable consummation." And this is the despair of every non-Christian philosophy or religion in the world. Evil cannot be removed by revolutionary process. There are no potentialities within that, unaided, can work a reformation. Sin cannot be civilized out of the heart and life. James Russell Lowell has aptly said: "There is a poison in the sores of Lazarus, against which Dives has no antidote."

With this marvelous success of evangelism, and its spirit of daring enterprise, we have demonstrated the best method of answering present day unbelief. The proclamation of truth, accompanied as it has been in all lands, by signs and wonders, gives triumphant answer to the boldest skepticism. While modern doubt is shifting its point of attack, the faithful preaching of Christ continues to work miracles of grace. And these are an end of argument. There is no appeal from a fact. A redeemed soul is worth more than a volume on apologetics. A living Lazarus, four days dead, is an infallible proof of resurrection power. The "Analogy" of Bishop Butler was a masterful, unanswerable argument; but the great revival which followed its publication, under the ministry of Whitfield, the Wesleys, and others, with its thousands of spiritual miracles, put to flight the armies of aliens. No charge against the insufficiency of revelation, or the inadequacy of Christian truth, or the inaccuracy of the Christian Scriptures, or the incredibility of Christianity's claims, can stand before the demonstrations of its power—the millions in all lands, redeemed thereby, all testifying that they do know. This indicates the true apologetic function of the preacher. He should not make the pulpit a professor's chair, nor follow lines of discussion before an ordinary congregation that belong to the pages of a Review. He more completely refutes infidelity by preaching Christ, the Saviour of the world.

Modern Missions have confirmed the faith of the Church in *man's common nature, in the unity of the race*. The readiness with which all races, under their multifarious civilizations, apprehend the gospel, and the identity of its effects upon personal and community life, reënforce the doctrine of man's common origin. "God has made of one blood all nations of men to dwell on the face of the earth." The distinguished Principal of Manchester College thus clearly states the doctrine in a singularly felicitous sentence: "If men differ in color, in blood, and in speech, they may still recognize common manhood, but as a matter of history common manhood has never been recognized save through common religion, and the only common religion which has made men recognize their common humanity has been that of Christ."

Christianity has but one law of life, and one standard of moral judgment for the high and the low, the wise and the unwise, the Greek and the barbarian. In intellectual merit there are wide distinctions, but the natural conscience of the race is about on the same level. The same standard is used in the moral appraisement of Anglo-Saxon and Fijian. Before the moral law there is no distinction of race, age, or nationality. Mr. Watkinson, in his Fernly Lecture, uses this language: " In the vast congregation assembled on Sabbath morning in the church of God throughout the earth all kinds of distinctions exist—distinctions of intellectual power, of culture, rank, wealth, age, country, calling. But when the Commandments are read, all these distinctions are ignored; a majestic standard of conduct is exalted with stern simplicity, and by this standard all alike must test themselves in the presence of God; no distinction exists except that of moral good and evil."

Now out of this unity comes moral fraternity. A common humanity necessitates a universal brotherhood. Of the witness of Christian Missions to this marvelous fact of the Christian religion, Dr. Fairbairn says: "It has made the civilized man feel that he and the savage are of one blood, that the savage is as dear to God as he is, has as vast capabilities, as boundless promise of being as his own nature can boast. The religion that has created this sense of kinship and duty is the true mother of man's faith in human fraternity."

Modern Missions have led the Church to an

awakened study of the doctrine of the Holy Spirit. An Anglican writer says: "The theology of the third Person is a department of sacred science in which the Church of England is confessedly weak." Dr. Pope says: "Indistinctness has prevailed on this subject in much of the theology of earlier and later times. The offices of the Holy Ghost have been obscured by exaggerations of sacramental efficiency, and his personal relations to the believer have been undervalued in many persons." Smeaton, an English writer, says: "Germany seems to have abandoned this whole field, as if it were no longer worthy of cultivation. There is not a single work in the whole compass of German literature on the office and work of the Holy Spirit, if we except the unfinished work of Kahnis."

The mighty signs of the century have brought the Church back to a new interpretation of the presence and office of the Holy Spirit. The miracles of the mission field—the Pentecosts reported from every land—have said to the Church: "This is that which hath been spoken by the prophet Joel; And it shall be in the last days, saith God, I will pour forth of my Spirit upon all flesh: . . . and it shall be, that whosoever shall call on the name of the Lord shall be saved."

These show that the bestowment of the Spirit is not the gift of a priest, but the act of God. And it is reasserted and abundantly illustrated in the history of Missions. The debased elevated, cannibals cured of their taste for human flesh, souls redeemed, nations transformed, attest the presence and omnipotence of the Holy Spirit.

To ascribe these to civilization, evolution, etc., would be to " blaspheme against the Holy Ghost." The history of Missions is the history of the Holy Spirit in the Church.

The Church has been given a clearer and wider recognition of the *Lordship of Jesus Christ.*

The history of Missions has been a successive unfolding and unveiling of the Son of God in his power and glory, a series of epiphanies of the risen and reigning Lord. His presence has been the one distinctive and glorious fact in the progress of the century. And, as Bishop Westcott says: " If anything can make us feel the nobility of life, it must be that in Christ we are enabled to recognize in the whole course of history a majestic spectacle of the action of divine love in which no failures and no willfulness of men can obliterate the signs and the promises of a presence of God."

The fuller recognition of Christ's kingship is a great gain. It means more perfect obedience, readier service, more cheerful endurance, and more trustful waiting. Attention has been called to the significant fact that the first word uttered by the awakened Saul of Tarsus was "Lord," and that word was the keynote of his splendid apostolic career.

Christ's ministry is *a personal ministry.* His government is a personal government. He takes personal command of the Church, and is himself the Great Captain of the world's salvation. "Lo, I am with you alway, even unto the end of the world." His immediate and constant presence is pledged. Of the Acts of the Apostles Canon Norris has said: "Surely one great purpose of this book is to teach us to recognize the personal government of Christ throughout his Church's history. Of that Church history of eighteen centuries, could it be written truly, this record of the first thirty years would be seen to be but a specimen page—the first of many pages, of which the last is not yet written. When the last page comes to be written, then shall we understand, as clearly as the writer of this page understood, the fulfillment of Christ's promise: 'Lo, I am with you alway, even unto the end of the world.' The history of Missions give 'many infallible proofs' of Christ's presence and personal administration."

Dr. Gordon thus happily states the doctrine of our Lord's personal and perpetual presence in the Church: "By Christ's ascent to the Father, and the Spirit's descent upon the disciples, the Church exchanged the presence of the Lord for his omnipresence; so that whereas in the time of his manifestation in the flesh he could be present only in one place at a time, in the time of his manifestation in the Spirit he could be present in all places at all times." Really the promise, "Lo, I am with you alway, even unto the end of the world," is without significance, if not an assurance that in an exceptional sense, in a very special manner, the omnipresent Lord will accompany the brave souls who go out in his name to disciple the nations."

Modern Missions have taught the Church new *lessons in the doctrine and duty of prayer*. Upon no other duty and privilege do the Scriptures bestow so frequent mention and lay such sacred emphasis. It is the most potential factor in personal life and the most efficient aid in spiritual service. To it the largest promises are made. We are assured that the divine response will only be measured by our asking. Dr. Cyrus Hamlin, a veteran missionary, says: "When Christians are knocking God is always opening doors."

Missions have certainly intensified and fostered *a spirit of prayer*. Indeed, the history of modern Missions is the history of answered prayer. The stupendous undertaking itself—in view of the vastness of the field, and the difficulties to be removed—has thrown the Church back upon God. There has been more simple reliance upon a divine arm, and more importunate pleading into the divine ear. It has been said that the published appeal of Jonathan Edwards for "a visible union of God's people in extraordinary prayer" was itself a turning point in modern history, especially in modern Missions. Dr. Pierson states the inspiring fact of history in this terse and striking phrase: "There has been no outpouring of the Spirit without a previous outpouring of souls to God." The new era of world-wide Missions was born of an awakened spirit of earnest prayer. Over a Christian and missionary "Home" for young English-American women in Paris are these words: "*Asked of God August 11, 1874; Given to God March 9, 1895.*" What thrilling eloquence in those brief words! But such inscriptions might be placed over a thousand doorways in the mission fields of the world.

From Tahite there comes an inspiring illustration: For sixteen years there seemed to be no promise of that field, no return for the expenditure of missionary labor. In that time of faithful toil and patient waiting there was but one conversion. Tribal wars raged, horrid rites were observed, disgusting idolatries were almost universal. The directors of the London Missionary Society were discussing the advisability of withdrawing their forces, and opening work in a more promising field. But some vigorously opposed abandonment, believed that the Holy Spirit would yet give them rich reward, and supported their faith by largely increased personal subscriptions. A season of prayer was appointed. Letters of encouragement were sent to the missionaries, in connection with which this remarkable coincidence, or rather providence, occurred: "*While the vessel was on her way to carry these letters to Tahiti another ship passed her in mid ocean which conveyed to Great Britain news that idolatry was overthrown in the island, and bore back to London the rejected idols of the people.* What a striking fulfillment of the divine promise: "Before they call, I will answer; and while they are yet speaking, I will hear!" And instances even more remarkable might be multiplied a thousandfold.

Missions have enriched the spiritual life of the Church. It deepens as it widens. An aggressive missionary zeal is necessary to conserve spiritual life at home. Wonderful words were those of the venerable Dr. Duff, Scotland's missionary hero: "The Church that ceases to evangelize will soon cease to be evangelical." They accord perfectly with that obverse statement of Prof. Bowne, in his "Logic of Religious Belief:" "Within the Church also, periods of rationalizing have always been periods of dearth and death." And both are suggestive comments on the law of spiritual development stated by our Lord himself: "To every one that hath shall be given, and he shall have abundance: but from him that hath not shall be taken away even that which he hath." And all history bears testimony to that momentous declaration. The evangelizing spirit must be kept warm and glowing, or indifferentism and deadness will ensue. A rationalizing pulpit preaches a lifeless gospel.

Those are suggestive and true words of the great Chillingworth: "Christianity is a strange commodity. The more you export, the more you have for home consumption." It is a law of spiritual life that he that giveth shall receive more abundantly, that "he that watereth shall be watered also himself."

The great Dr. Andrew Fuller, as quoted by Dr. John Harris, thus wrote to a friend:

There was a period of my ministry marked by the most pointed systematic effort to comfort my serious people; but the more I tried to comfort them the more they complained of doubts and darkness. . . . I knew not what to do nor what to think, for I had done my best to comfort the mourners in Zion. At this time it pleased God to direct my attention to the claims of the perishing heathen in India. I felt that we had been living for ourselves, and not caring for their souls. I spoke as I felt. My serious people wondered and wept over their past inattention to the subject. . . . We met and prayed for the heathen; met and considered what could be done among ourselves for them; met and did what we could. And, while all this was going on, the lamentations ceased. The sad became cheerful, and the desponding calm. And I, instead of having to study how to comfort my flock, was myself comforted by them. They were drawn out of themselves. God blessed them while they tried to be a blessing.

Missions have demonstrated the great principle of Christ's kingdom, so clearly enunciated, that we get from the Lord as we give to the Lord. "There is that scattereth, and yet increaseth." This is not a premium upon a low, commercial aspect of the gospel, no assurance that an invested penny will return us a pound; but the gain comes in a larger manhood and in richer and increased spiritual life, though history testifies that an investment in Missions has brought large commercial returns. The mission to the Sandwich Islands is said to have cost $5,000,000, while the trade with that country amounted to

$16,000,000 in six years—making the interest for two years exceed the entire principal. The great gain is in *enlarged power* at home.

A Church cannot live on its history. Serene contentment with the past is sure prophecy of decadence in the future. It emasculates spiritual manhood, weakens the inspirations of constraining love. What a striking illustration have we in the Copts of Egypt! Once numerous and powerful, standing bravely against Mohammedan cruelty and tyranny—adding some of the noblest names to the martyrology of the centuries—they have ceased to be aggressive, complacently satisfied with the past, until they have grown weak in numbers and weaker in all the elements of Christian life and character.

The Church lives as it imparts life. It strengthens as it expands. Its life deepens as it spreads. "A Christianity which is not aggressive becomes regressive. A state of inaction sinks into a state of degeneration. A reclining Church soon becomes a declining Church." And again it has been said that "a Christianity which simply nourishes itself soon loses its power."

With the extension of Christ's kingdom into the distant regions and among the most degraded peoples, additional emphasis is given to another great

Christian truth, *that service to man is consecration to God;* and that really the only way to serve God is to help man. " He serves Jesus best who serves the neediest of men in their greatest need," are the discriminating words of a great thinker. The divine exhortation is: "Bear ye one another's burdens, and so fulfill the law of Christ." And the law of Christ was eminently the law of his own life. It inspired his every parable, it wrought his every miracle, it directed his every journey, it commanded his every thought, it consumed his every energy, it accomplished his tragic death, and ultimated in his glorious resurrection and transcendent, perpetual priesthood. God, who is self-existent and infinite in his perfections, has no lack that we can supply, has no need that appeals to our sympathy. But the needs of men are *his* needs, their sorrows are *his* heaviest burdens. By ministering to them, we serve God.

And how this law of service dignifies human life and glorifies our Christian religions. Buddha's boast was: "I am no man's servant." Jesus said: "If any man would be great among you, let him be the servant of all." As illustrative of this Christly spirit, how beautiful is that story of Baron Von Welz, the forerunner of Swartz and Carey, who, renouncing his titles and estates, went to Dutch Guiana, and after a time filled a missionary's grave. He said: "What to me is the title 'well born,' when I am one born again in Christ? What is to me the title 'lord,' when I desire to be a servant of Christ? What to me to be called 'your Grace,' when I have need of God's grace, help, and succor? All these vanities I will away with, and everything besides I will lay at the feet of Jesus, my dearest Lord, that I may have no hindrance in serving him aright?"

The history of Christian Missions has been a divine illustration of this great law of life.

Missions have brought *the Christian world into closer union.* A distinguishing and happy feature of modern Church life—"a sign alike of rejuvenescence and of ripening"—is the awakened instinct of oneness among the Churches of Christ, and the articulate craving for, and the earnest feeling after, some feasible manifestation of that oneness in the face of an unbelieving, warring world. Children of the same Father, brethren of the same Elder Brother, with the same spiritual blood flowing in our veins, animated by the same impulse, journeying to the same home, temples of the same Holy Ghost, we have fellowship with each other. This fellowship oversteps the narrow bounds of land and sea, and overleaps the lines of race, sect, party, and nation. It merges "the clan into the country," the race into the oneness of the world's blessed brotherhood, and the sect into the universal kingdom of our one Lord and Saviour. And with this all-embracing and constraining love there comes a sense of divine indebtedness to the wide world—to Greek and barbarian, to the wise and unwise.

To this growing spirit of Christian comity and unity the modern missionary movement has made the largest contribution. In the presence of a common foe Christians stand close together. Minor differences are forgotten, points of agreement are multiplied and emphasized, and the unity for which our Lord prayed is seen to be the essential condition of the world's evangelization. His prayer, "That they all may be one," was in order "that *the world* may believe that thou hast sent me."

LECTURE VI.

LESSONS FROM SOME MASTER MISSIONARIES.

VI.

LESSONS FROM SOME MASTER MISSIONARIES.

THE characters of the apostles are as instructive as their acts; their lives, as inspiring as their labors. What God wrought in them is as important a lesson as what God wrought through them. We want to see the messenger while we hear his message, and the character of the messenger is often the best commentary on his message. So, back of the Acts, marvelous though they be in our eyes, we fix most eager gaze on the apostles themselves. And as we study the men we better understand their wonderful words and mighty deeds. Probably the grandest product of the first Christian century was the majestic and many-sided character of the apostle Paul. Everywhere, his words and works—his inspiring sermons and apostolic achievements—are overshadowed by his towering personality. We trace with intense eagerness the track of his missionary movements, and recount with thrilling interest the marvelous incidents of his providential history, but never for a moment lose sight of the massive figure of the masterful leader himself. And all the elements in that great character are of divine development. God developed him, while he used him. He is the Holy Spirit's product of a missionary career.

So modern Missions, under the administration of that same Holy Spirit, have developed great characters. While the heathen have been redeemed, the laborers have been ennobled. The message has transfigured the messengers. The great field, which is the world, has not only produced sheaves of heathen converts, but harvests of heroic character and apostolic achievement. The workers have been proven while the work has prospered. It is the aim of this lecture to study the characters and careers of some pioneer missionaries of the century, and try to ascertain the lessons that they were designed to teach the Church.

Renan said that "the true miracle of nascent Christianity was the spirit of Jesus strongly grafted into his disciples: the spirit of sweetness, of self-abnegation, of forgetfulness of the present; that unique pursuit of inward joy which kills ambition." That spirit, grafted into Christians of this day and in every land, is perpetuating "the true miracle of nascent Christianity." And in no single class of Christians is that spirit so "strongly grafted," and by whom "the true miracle of nascent Christianity" is more wonderfully wrought than the missionaries of the various fields.

Mr. Lecky, in his "History of European Morals," has said: "One great cause of the success of Christianity was that it produced more heroic actions and formed more upright men than any other creed." And to this crowning demonstration of Christianity modern missionaries have made the wealthiest contributions. Their names have become the synonyms for the highest virtues and the noblest achievements. For lofty character, undaunted courage, quenchless zeal, entire self-abnegation, and perfect consecration to one supreme beneficent purpose, there are no nobler illustrations than the men and women of moral greatness and apostolic devotion, whose lives have been made a freewill offering to the Christless nations. Dr. John Harris did not hesitate to say that they had "served and saved the character of the Church." Dr. Lawrence, a high authority, who spent years in a personal study of mission fields, felt constrained to say that "the consecrated list of the heroes of faith and the saints of love whose light shines most conspicuous in their march across the lands and the ages is more thronged with the names of missionaries than with those of any other class." And having myself inspected the work in many lands, I most heartily agree with the suggestion that the work itself brings compensation and blessings in the way of character and grace which there is no space to mention. Indeed, Theodore Parker went so far as to say that, " Had the whole missionary work resulted in nothing more than the building up of such a character as Adoniram Judson, it would be worth all it has cost."

Religion is tested not only by the " fitness of its conceptions," but by *"the force of its inspirations."* Behind the great ideas—the doctrines—the truths of religion must be its spirit—its spirit that throbs with life and has the quiver of power. This is the measure of its value and virtue as a reforming and transforming power. Not every correct conception has the force of an inspiration; not every sublime truth stirs the soul to action. They touch no emotions, they awaken no desires, they compel no heroic endeavor. The doctrine of gravity is absolutely true and universally accepted, but has no power to kindle enthusiasm. So there are religions that are avowedly limited, with no spirit of enterprise or power of propagation; and yet others that seek universal extension, but have exhausted the force of their inspiration.

But Christianity is essentially missionary. Its very words are spirit and life. It not only gratifies and satisfies; it inspires. We no sooner embrace it than we have a joyous impulse to communicate it. Interest in others is enkindled. And the growth of this spiritual concern for the unsaved is the measure of our religion. The love that prompted our Lord's coming constrains our going. Under its impulse we proclaim the truth he revealed, we propagate what he preached, we continue what he began. On the contrary, unconcern for others is an impeachment of the Christian's faith, an abrogation of the Christian's commission, a reversal of his sacred mission. So a true religion must not only teach us what to do, but implant the inspiring force which will create the desire to do it. "Cold illumination is not enough; the fire must be burning upon the altar." Religion must *inspire* as well as *instruct*.

Now, I do not think it too much to say that the *inspiring* force of Christianity has been most strikingly displayed in the lives and labors of Christian missionaries. Their tender solicitude for the Christless millions, their divine eagerness to fly to their relief, their unremitting labors to arouse the conscience of the Church, their sublime courage which no dangers could arrest, their heroic fortitude which no privations could exhaust, and their conquering faith which the shadows of the grave could not obscure, are the world's grandest expression of the dynamics of Christianity. No disappointments or difficulties have for a moment checked their efforts or curbed their restless spirits. We discern the inspiring force in St. Paul's life as we follow him in his tireless missionary wanderings on land and sea. Amid poverty and persecution he labored with unremitting zeal to bring men to Jesus. So stirred was his great soul by this inspiring force, and so enraptured by the vision of the field, that he arose and exclaimed: "*I can but preach.*" The full heart and fired brain had to speak. The unlocked fountain would flow, even if it had to cut a channel for the majestic sweep of its liberated waters. Again he said, as if in seeming explanation of his fervent and restless zeal: "The love of Christ *constraineth* me." And when opposition grew more intense, and the storm of persecution began to beat upon him in pitiless fury, sustained by an unshaken purpose and impelled by this divine desire for the world's redemption, he cried out, above the roar of the tempest: "*None of these things move* me." It was intimate acquaintance with his Lord, and profound, prayerful study of the desperate needs of the world, that lifted the great apostle into masterful leadership and fired his soul with the spirit of glorious conquest. And that same sublime passion, that same disinterested love of humanity, has been reincarnated in the missionary heroes and heroines of this missionary century. To all lands they have eagerly gone in this Pauline spirit, attempting great things for God and expecting great things from God.

So Christlike have been their lives and so divine the virtues they have illustrated that the names of great missionaries have become synonymous with certain Christian graces. The eloquent Dr. John Harris thus describes the characteristics of some noble names:

> Eliot, Zeisberger, and Brainerd are but other names for indefatigable labor and enterprise, and self-consuming ardor. We think of Swartz, and the might of character. The accomplished youth, panting to live for Christ in distant lands, but derided as a visionary, thinks of Martyn and takes courage. Pious and disinterested poverty reads of Carey, and emerges from its humble cell to perform labors which excite the devout thanksgiving of the Church. Faith looks at the origin and early history of the Moravian Mission, and, undismayed by the scantiness of her human resources, girds up the loins of her mind, and addresses herself to her task afresh. Their biography is creating for the Church a literature of its own. Their example is reproducing itself in a second race. To the influence of Brainerd the Church is chiefly indebted, under God,

for the labors of Milne. The pious father gives their names to his sons as a title of excellence and an incitement to attain it. Their zeal for God has kindled a fire at which numbers are lighting their torches. And thus, in various ways, have they given ardor to holy activity, and multiplied the power of truth; while the Church below unites with the Church above in glorifying God in them.

One assurance has been given fresh emphasis in the history of modern Missions: that the Holy Spirit as distinctly calls and anoints for service to-day as he designated and sent forth apostles in the early Church. The history of apostolic Missions opens with these words: "The Holy Ghost said, Separate me Barnabas and Saul for the work whereunto I have called them. . . . So they, being sent forth by the Holy Ghost, departed unto Seleucia; and from thence they sailed to Cyprus." And in the same way and by the same authoritative voice the Holy Ghost has separated and sent forth missionaries into the world. Barnabas and Saul were not more divinely anointed and appointed than were Coke and Carey and Calvert. Without discussing the nature of this call and the manner of its communication, without inquiring into the "mysterious interworkings of the Spirit of God and the spirit of man," I simply state the fact that the Holy Ghost's oversight of the Church is in nothing more manifest than in his distinct designation and sending forth of laborers in the harvest fields of the world.

Another fact attests the purpose and presence of the Holy Spirit in modern Missions: *the marvelous adaptation of the workers to the work.*

It is most instructive to study the individualities and gifts of the special agents God employed in the great crises of the world's history. The qualities and characteristics of the men as much indicate the purpose of God as their divine call to service. When the abominations of Baal worship were to be overthrown and the tyrannous rule of Ahab broken, God needed a prophet of fire and terror; so he went into the wilderness for Elijah the Tishbite, and clothed him with majesty almost divine. But after the prophet of woe, he needed a pastor, after the destroyer a builder, after the shiver of earthquake and the sweep of storm and fire he wanted a "still small voice;" so he threw a mantle over the shoulders of the gentle Elisha, and sent him out to comfort the people. And when the fullness of time had come, when immediate preparation was to be made for the coming of the King, God needed not "a reed shaken by the wind," not "a man clothed in soft raiment," but a man of decision, of hardihood, of lofty courage; so he called John the Baptist and sent him out as "a voice crying in the wilderness." And that same marvelous discrimination of the Holy Spirit has been abundantly illustrated in the call and appointment of modern missionaries.

It was not by accident that Adoniram Judson went to Burmah, instead of to India, as he had first planned. In him were the very qualities needed for planting the gospel and founding the Church in the far-off land. And how perfectly adapted was William Carey to the stupendous task assigned him by the Holy Spirit in Northern India! A man of less steady nerve would have yielded to fierce opposition, and a heart of less heroic purpose would have gone down under the strain of hopeless waiting. And by his marvelous power of acquiring language he soon laid the foundations for a Christian literature in India, and compelled the East India Company, which at first refused him civil protection, to call him to the professorship of Sanskrit in the University of Calcutta. In every feature of his character there was a special purpose, and every event of his life was a divine providence. And so of Morrison in China, and Moffat in Africa, and John Williams in the South Seas, and Calvert in Fiji, and Mackay in Uganda, and hundreds of others whose names and worthy deeds are written in the chronicles of the skies.

And modern missionaries have shown the Christ spirit in their eagerness *to serve God's neediest children in their greatest need*. Paul, the model missionary, gives us the inspiring motive of his wonderful career in these words, addressed to the Church at Rome: " Yea, so have I strived to preach the gospel, *not where Christ was named*, lest I should build upon another man's foundation; but as it is written, To whom he was not spoken of, they shall see: and they that have not heard shall understand." He had a divine impatience to save the lost. His ministry was to the most needy, those to " whom Christ was not named." The more desperate and neglected their condition, the tenderer was his solicitude, and the more intense his desire for their relief. " The wide unfilled provinces of his apostolate ever called him on."

That example has been emulated in every mission field. Illustrations might be given by the thousand of those who were not in the least behind the great apostle in consuming zeal for the lowliest. Robert Morrison, the apostle of China, offered this prayer: " My desire is, O Lord, to engage where laborers are most wanted." William Milne, twice rejected as a missionary, asked to be allowed to accompany Dr. Morrison to China as his servant. He became a great missionary, and is spoken of in history as "that excellent man, whose talents were surprising, whose labors were incessant, whose whole life was devoted to his Saviour." Pao, who became the apostle of the island of Lifu, was landed upon Mare, forty miles away. When he saw the vessel sailing away, and impatient of delay in reaching his field, he cried aloud: "Do not I know about God? O, let me go and tell the heathen what I know!" Then, refusing to await the return of the ship, he sprang into a canoe, and with a Bible in one hand and a paddle in the other "shot like an arrow over the crested wave of a dangerous sea." With one companion, he reached the island in safety, and began his evangelistic work. In twelve years cannibals were civilized, whole villages burned their idols, and nine thousand persons professed faith in the Son of God. And hundreds of others have shown like heroic purpose to go down into the depths of the world's sorest need.

The Czarina of Russia, widow of the late Emperor, some years before his death, uttered words that contain a beautiful lesson. In speaking of the constant peril of the Czar's life, she said: "I am thankful to the Nihilists for one thing. They have made me love my husband dearly. Our home life has become so different since I began to look upon him as though he were under sentence of death. You can't think how deeply this menaced state attaches me to him." Anxiety for his personal safety, and knowledge of the fact that bitter malignity shadowed his every footstep, and exhausted all human and inhuman ingenuity to accomplish his death, awoke every secret and latent sentiment of her heart toward him. It opened an undiscovered fountain of affection, and made the indifferent bride a tender, watchful, loving companion. She became to him more a wife than a queen.

So peril increases attachment. It awakens and displays the abandon of love. And this is true in things spiritual. The soul's danger intensifies concern. It was this that made Jeremiah a prophet of tears. The dreadful sins of Israel, and the doom which he knew was impending, almost broke his sympathetic heart. In his agony of anxiety he cried out: "Is there *no* balm in Gilead? Is there *no* physician there?" And it is this knowledge of the degradation and doom of heathen peoples that has written the brilliant history of modern missionary heroism.

Missionaries have given the Church some *new lessons in personal consecration.* They have illustrated what Paul meant when he said: "For me to live is Christ." Count Zinzendorf, the head of the Moravian Church, said: "I have but one passion, and that is He, only He." Henry Martyn, who fell into an early missionary grave, a sacrifice to his consuming zeal, said: "I see no business in life but the work of Jesus Christ, neither do I desire any employment to all eternity but his service." A Moravian missionary sold himself into slavery that he might preach the gospel more effectively to the slaves. "That is what incarnation means," says a distinguished writer. And no apostle of all the ages has ever exhibited a spirit of more perfect self-abnegation than that saintly missionary in India, who uttered this prayer: "O Lord, if thou canst not make me a soul-winner here, set me aside from this calling, and appoint others who will save these millions." Such self-debasement in order to the redemption of the nations demonstrates the fact, as the author of "Ecce Homo!" happily phrases it, that "the verb to love really has an imperative mood."

A missionary to the Dark Continent gave utterance to this noble sentiment: "I think it is with African Missions as with the building of a great bridge. You know how many stones have to be buried in the earth, all unseen, for a foundation.

If Christ wants me to be one of the unseen stones, lying in an African grave, I am content."

So perfect has been the consecration of these later apostles, and so obedient their ardent spirits, that they have readily discerned a Providence in the most discouraging events in their lives. They have found in a seeming disaster the divine assurance of speedier and grander victory by another line of battle and a different character of campaign. The humble Moravians thus interpreted their persecutions and consequent dispersion. They said: "If we have been cast out and rendered homeless, it must be by the divine will that we shall become ambassadors for the Master, who had not where to lay his head." And so with ready and cheerful obedience they have gone to the ends of the earth. Count Zinzendorf once said to a young Moravian Christian: "Will you go to Greenland?" "Yes." "When?" "To-morrow, if the shoemaker can finish the boots I have ordered."

Another characteristic of missionary consecration *is the joy of service.* Constraining love becomes a sustaining grace. Labor is not weariness, burdens seem light, and the joy of service eliminates every element of sacrifice. Brainerd so loved the heathen that without their salvation nothing could make him happy. James Calvert, though in labors abundant and perils oft among the cannibals of Fiji, said: "We had no *night* of toil; God was with us from the first, and all along." Dr. John Talmage, of China, who recently died after more than forty-five years of service, said: "The missionary of Christ knows no sacrifice. His work is all joy, nothing but joy." Mackay, who has been called the "St. Paul of Uganda," wrote these words, which ought to inspire in us a deeper consecration to God: "I don't consider it a self-sacrifice, as some count it, to come here as a pioneer of Christ and civilization. I would not exchange my place for all the world. A powerful race here is to be won for Christ, men are to be brought to love God and one another, and in order to do that, institutions that have lasted for ages are to be uprooted, and wisdom has to be implanted. Who would not give his life for such a noble work as that?"

On October 7, 1805, Carey, Marshman, and Ward drew their famous "Form of Agreement," sometimes called "Carey's Covenant," which evidences their apostolic purpose and singular consecration. It seems to have been born from above —was inspired by the Holy Ghost. Dr. George Smith, the historian of Missions, says that it "embodies the divine principles of all Protestant scriptural Missions, and is still a manual to be daily pondered by every missionary, and by every Church and society which may send a missionary forth." Once a year it was publicly read in every station, as a reminder of missionary vows and an occasion for their renewal. As has been said, this solemn compact sounds like an apostolic document:

It is absolutely necessary

1. That we set an infinite value upon immortal souls.
2. That we gain all information of the snares and delusions in which these heathen are held.
3. That we abstain from all those things which would increase their prejudices against the gospel.
4. That we watch all opportunities for doing good.
5. That we keep to the example of Paul, and make the great subject of our preaching Christ the crucified.
6. That the natives should have an entire confidence in us and feel quite at home in our company.
7. That we build up and watch over the souls that may be gathered.
8. That we form our native brethren to usefulness, fostering every kind of genius and cherishing every gift and grace in them, especially advising the native churches to choose their own pastors and deacons from among their own countrymen.
9. That we labor with all our might in forwarding translations of the sacred Scriptures in the languages of India.
10. That we establish native free schools, and recommend these establishments to other Europeans.

11. That we be constant in prayer and the cultivation of personal religion, to fit us for the discharge of these laborious and unutterably important labors. Let us often look at Brainerd in the woods of America, pouring out his very soul before God for the perishing heathen, without whose salvation nothing could make him happy.

12. That we give ourselves unreservedly to this glorious cause. Let us never think that our time, our gifts, our strength, our families, or even the clothes we wear, are our own. Let us sanctify them all to God and his cause. O that he may sanctify us for his work! No private family ever enjoyed a greater portion of happiness than we have done since we resolved to have all things in common. If we are enabled to persevere, we may hope that multitudes of converted souls will have reason to bless God to all eternity for sending his gospel into this country.

The sufferings and martyrdom of missionaries recall the age and Acts of the Apostles. The privations of the first missionaries to Greenland are almost unparalleled, and their discouragements to less heroic spirits would have been appalling. We are told that they at times could only satisfy hunger on shellfish and seaweed; they occasionally had to eat the remnants of tallow candles, and considered themselves fortunate if they "had train oil to mix with their scant morsel of oatmeal." And yet they stood firmly at their posts and labored on —only at last to be richly rewarded. In Western Greenland it is said that there is not a single pagan left. Dr. Kane gave this testimony: "The missionaries have been so far successful among the natives of Greenland that there are but few of them who are not Christians."

Six hundred missionaries sleep in the soil of India. West Africa has been called the "White Man's Grave," but the deadly climate has never deterred brave men and women from going there to labor and to die. The Church Missionary Society alone lost fifty-three missionaries in twenty years. And in all the fields they sleep in honored graves.

Mexico has been a field of blood. Its soil has been drenched with the blood of martyrs. Within a few years not less than sixty were brutally slain, for no other crime than telling of a Saviour's love.

Missionaries have given new meaning to *the grace of patient waiting*. There is no higher expression of faith than that which, having done all, is able cheerfully to stand—after laborious toil can "stand *still* and see the salvation of the Lord." We wonder at the sublime hopefulness of the missionaries.

When Judson had been eighteen years in Burmah some one wrote and asked: "What of the prospect?" The great-souled apostle replied: "Bright as the promises of God." To others it seemed that not a seed would grow, that it was all stony ground. The heavens shone like brass upon the blistered soil, with never a cloud so large as a man's hand to tell of a coming shower. Yet they confidently trusted and patiently waited. It is a strange coincidence that it was seven years before Carey in India, Judson in Burmah, Morrison in China, Moffat in Africa, or Henry Richards on the Congo, each baptized his first convert. How severely their faith must have been tested! Think of a husbandman looking anxiously upon the same field every day for seven weary years before he discovered that a single seed had begun to germinate. Does all prophetic and apostolic history show sublimer endurance or more unfaltering faith? Jeremiah, though given repeated and miraculous assurances, became at times discouraged almost to the point of despair. His entreaties had been so long unheeded, his brotherly sympathies so rudely repulsed, and his solemn warnings so defiantly mocked and ridiculed, that he lost hope for his people, and was tempted to lose faith in his message. So great was his discouragement that the prophet cried out: "I will not make mention of him, nor speak any more in his name." But happily, just then came back the vivid memory of his divine call and consecration—of the blessed promise of strength for every hour of need—and as the cloud lifted, he girded up his faith and exclaimed: "But his word was in mine heart as a burning fire shut up in my bones."

But a consecrated missionary, however discouraged, never gets to the point of despair. He is an enlightened optimist. In all the East I did not hear a doleful tone or a discouraging word. And those who had been longest in the field seemed the most enthusiastic. There was no undervaluing of opposing forces, no underestimating the strength of the enemy, no idle sentiment about a millennial dawn without further sacrifice and struggle; but they firmly believed that God's enduement of power would bring final and glorious victory. In all there was the same hopeful spirit, the ardent expectation of a near and abundant harvest.

The unfaltering faith of the missionaries has also sustained and cheered the confidence and hope of the Church at home. It should be just the reverse. The Church should comfort and encourage them amid the gloom and loneliness of heathen lands. But they have had not only to endure the hardness and even horrors of the field—they have had to buttress the faith and sympathy of the Church. There are missions that have enjoyed Pentecosts of the Spirit, and become strong, self-extending centers of spiritual evangelism, which would have been abandoned had not the missionary's hope been stronger than the enfeebled faith of the Church. A signal illustration comes from China. The Church Missionary Society opened a station in the province of Fuh-kien in 1850. Eleven years passed without a single convert. During that time of anxious waiting three missionaries died at their posts. In the tenth year, "without one single conversion or prospect of such a thing," the home Board was about to abandon the field. For ten years they had come seeking fruit and found none. But yielding to the importunity of Mr. Smith, their only missionary left, they deferred final action. The brave-hearted and Spirit-baptized apostle, who would rather have been buried with his comrades than flee the field, wrote home as follows: "I hope that a brighter day is about to dawn upon us. There are three men whom I really look upon as honest inquirers." Those who compute the cost of converts in dollars would say: "Why this waste?" After ten long, toilsome years, and only three that even "look" like honest inquirers! But the heroic missionary had the full assurance of faith, and history vindicated his fidelity. In 1891 there were 8,500 Christian adherents, one-third of whom were devout communicants, embraced in their one hundred and fifty stations and out stations.

Another fact which indicates the seemingly impossible work to be accomplished, and also illustrates the sublime faith and heroism of missionaries, is the morally degraded condition of the heathen. It is true that there is a natural Sinai in every human heart, but centuries of ignorance and superstition have almost entirely effaced the characters written therein. The difficulty is thus stated by David Livingstone, who spoke by authority of long experience and accurate knowledge: "There is a work to be done by missionaries which people in Christian lands hardly dream of. They have to create a moral sense before they can appeal to it—to arouse their conscience before they can look to its admonitions to enforce their teachings. Their consciences are seared, and moral perceptions blasted. Their memories scarcely retain anything we teach them. So low have they sunk that the plainest texts in the whole Bible cannot be understood by them. It is hard, until one goes to a heathen country, to realize how much civilization owes to Christianity."

They have brought us back to the basal fact that faith in his message is the true source of the preacher's inspiration. One of the distinguishing characteristics of these heroic disciples, recalling and emulating the missionary zeal and spirit of St.

Paul himself, is their unquestioning faith in their message. While we are hesitant, they are hopeful. After the clearest promise of our message's power—that it is by "the foolishness of preaching" that the nations are to be redeemed, that the truth can make any man and all men free—there is a strange skepticism as to its immediate effects. There is not a confident expectation of results, an assurance of victories gained by the truth's simple and faithful announcement. There is too little disappointment if the power of conviction and conversion is not seen.

Bishop Thoburn admits that the conversion of Hindoos during the delivery of his message marked a distinct experience, a spiritual epoch in his life as a missionary. He said: "I have long since ceased to marvel at them. The real wonder is that I should have preached nearly fifteen years before discerning that the ambassador of Jesus Christ, intrusted with the ministry of reconciliation, is really able *through his message* to do that which he is sent to accomplish." That faith is the condition of heroic endeavor and endurance. Convincing speech is the inspiration of profound conviction of truth.

Dean Millman has truly said: "No Pelagian ever has or ever will work a reformation. He who is destined for such a work must have a full conviction that God is acting, directly, immediately, consciously, and therefore with irresistible power, *upon* and *through* him."

One of the four principal objections to Foreign Missions is that " they are and have been in the hands of unfit and incapable men." If that be true, the Church ought either to improve the character of her workmen or else abandon the field. But is there real ground for such an objection? Were those lacking in fitness and capacity who bravely pioneered the cause of Missions in the various fields? And are their successors, now prosecuting the work so heroically begun, no better equipped for the needs of such a stupendous enterprise? As a matter of fact they have been the great scholars of the century, and have made the largest contributions to the languages and literature of the world. The construction of language and establishing a literature " have been taken in hand, not by *science*, so proud of her powers, not by *commerce*, that celebrated civilizer, not by the European colonial policy, so much belauded as the educator of barbarians, but by the despised mission, wherever she has planted her foot amid barbarism."

This mastery of the dense ignorance of the heathen is the monumental achievement of the missionaries. They have first to impart Christian ideas, and then construct a language with which to impart them. Such a task seems almost hopeless. But by the ingenuity and inventiveness of faith this barrier is made to give way, and in every land the statement is verified: "The entrance of thy Word giveth light." No wonder Mr. Darwin said: "The lesson of the missionary is the enchanter's wand."

As to the fitness and capacity of missionaries, I give the judgments of two of the foremost scholars, who testify that which they do know. A distinguished scientist, Lewis H. Morgan, pays this generous tribute to missionaries:

> There is no class of men upon the earth, whether considered as scholars, as philanthropists, or as gentlemen, who have earned for themselves a more distinguished reputation. Their labors, their self-denials, and their endurance in the work to which they have devoted their time and their abilities, are worthy of admiration. Their contributions to history, to ethnology, to philosophy, to geography, and to religious literature, form a lasting monument to their fame. The renown which encircles their names falls as a wreath of honor upon the name of their country.

Dr. Cust, in "The Languages of Africa," is alike generous in judgment:

> Let me turn away from the subject of language, and say one farewell word of the missionaries, those good and unselfish

men who, for a high object, have sacrificed careers which might have been great and honored in their own countries, and have gone forth to live in hovels, and sometimes to die; who, as it were, in the course of their striking hard on the anvil of evangelization, their own proper work, have emitted bright sparks of linguistic light, which have rendered luminous a region previously shrouded in darkness, and their sparks have kindled a corresponding feeling of warmth in the hearts of great, and to them personally unknown, scholars, working in their studies in Vienna, Berlin, or some great German university; scholars who, alas! cared little for the object of the missionaries' going forth, but rejoiced exceedingly at the wonderful, unexpected, epoch-making results of their quiet labors.

Mr. Denby, our American Minister at Peking, said: "Believe nobody who sneers at the missionaries. . . . They are heroes and heroines as truly as Grant or Sheridan, Nelson or Farragut."

The high character and consecrated unselfishness of the missionaries have overcome native prejudice and won their admiration for the Christian religion. Prof. Christleib has said: "The moral influence of Christianity and Christians in China, and also in India, is almost wholly sustained through the missionaries alone."

Addressing a missionary in India, a high-caste Hindoo said: "You missionaries are the only persons in whom we really have confidence." One of the most suggestive instances is the influence of Father Swartz, the great missionary of South India. Native princes were his warmest friends, and when all other foreigners were distrusted and detested he was honored and followed. "Do not send to me any of your agents," said Hyder Ali, in his message to the Council at Madras, "for I do not trust their words or treaties; but if you wish me to listen to your proposals, send to me the missionary Swartz, of whose character I hear so much from every one. Him will I receive and trust."

As illustrative of the doctrines and principles herein set forth, I give in brief outline a sketch of a few devoted and noted missionaries in the several great fields of the East.

Francis Xavier.

Whatever criticisms may be justly passed upon the methods of Francis Xavier as a missionary, and thereby account for the comparative prominence of his labors, he must rank, in spirit and consecration, with the greatest apostles of the ages. He was of noble Portuguese birth—connected with the house of Bourbon and the royal family of Navarre. Ardently devoted to Ignatius Loyola, he was one of the small company that laid the foundations of the Jesuit order—which, by the way, originated in an agreement between seven young men to devote themselves to the conversion of the heathen world to Christianity. It fell to

Xavier's lot to be the missionary pioneer of India. He went out the guest of a viceroy, and clothed with ample authority, from both the pope and the King of Portugal. His zeal knew no abatement and his labors were prodigious. At times the degradation of the heathen so overwhelmed him that he became the Jeremiah of his age. "O rock, rock, when wilt thou open to my Master?" On another occasion he uttered this passionate cry: "It often comes into my mind to go around all the universities of Europe crying like a madman to all the learned men whose learning is greater than their charity, 'Ah, what a multitude of souls are through your fault shut out of heaven.'"

His intense desire for the speedy evangelization of the nations, coupled with his exaggerated estimate of baptism as a means of conversion, caused him to invoke civil power to compel the heathen to become Christian. In a letter to the king he said: "I very earnestly desire that you should take an oath, invoking most solemnly the name of God, that in case any governor thus neglects to spread the faith, he shall, on his return to Portugal, be punished by close imprisonment for many years, and all his goods and possessions shall be sold and devoted to works of charity. In order that none may flatter themselves that this is but an idle threat, you must declare as plainly as possible that you will accept no excuses that may be offered; but that the only way of escaping your wrath and obtaining your favor is to make as many Christians as possible in the countries over which they rule. . . . So long as the viceroys and governors are not urged by the fear of disgrace and fine to make many Christians, your Majesty must not hope that the preaching of the gospel will meet with great success in India."

In his sanctified impatience to give all nations the gospel — feeling his divine indebtedness to Greek and barbarian, to the wise and unwise — he left India and sailed eastward as far as Japan. His five years in that island kingdom were in many respects the most faithful in his entire evangelistic career. From Japan he went to China, and in the midst of busy preparation for what he thought would be the greatest work of his life, in the greatest mission field of the world, he died December 2, 1552, at Macao, not very far from the city of Canton. "No companion was near to whom he could breathe out his dying thoughts, no priest gave him the last offices of the Church, or committed his body to a Christian grave."

Now after three centuries have passed, his fame as an earnest Christian abides, though few results of his labors survive. He was unwise as a missionary leader, and had some false conceptions of the best methods to promote God's work; but for purity of purpose, and saintliness of life, and earnestness of effort, and restlessness of zeal, he will ever deserve to rank among apostolic forerunners of this missionary century.

Christian Frederick Swartz, the Apostle of Southern India.

As Dr. John Harris observed, the name of Swartz stands for "might of character." He possessed a singular combination of qualities for masterful leadership. Not by self-assertion, but by a common impulse he was accorded kingship among men. Amid heathen people, hostile to his religion, he commanded not only highest respect, but the greatest veneration, and everywhere exercised almost unchallenged authority. This marvelous quality evidenced the striking providence in his appointment to India.

In 1726, in Sonnenburg, Prussia, a Christian wife and mother when dying thus whispered to her weeping husband: "I have dedicated our youngest son to God for such service as he shall appoint. Assure me that when he hears the Lord's call you will not discourage it." That youngest son was Christian Frederick Swartz, who early gave his heart to his mother's God. Returning from Halle, where he was educated, he told his father that the Lord had called him to missionary work in India. It is said that "the father retired to the chamber hallowed by the mother's saintly death, and after three days' struggle with his widower-heart, he yielded his youngest born upon the altar of God." In 1750 Swartz joined the Danish mission at Tranquebar, and began his wonderful missionary career.

His linguistic attainments were remarkable. He had rare and ready power for acquiring language. This enabled him speedily to speak in the language of the people, and gave him great power over the congregations that gathered to his ministry. His first sermon was preached in Tamil within four months after landing in the country. "Father Swartz," as he was reverently called, was for years the most influential man in all India. On the tablet to his memory in the church at Tajore, erected by a native prince, are these words: "His unspotted probity and purity of life alike commanded the reverence of the Christian, Mohammedan, and Hindoo; for sovereign princes, Hindoo and Mohammedan, selected this humble pastor as the medium of political negotiation with the British Government, and the very marble that here records his virtues was raised by the liberal affection and esteem of the Rajah of Tanjore, Maha Raja Sinfogee."

In his letter to Lord Cornwallis, Gen. Fullerton says: "On our second march we were visited by the Rev. Mr. Swartz, whom your lordship and the Board requested to proceed to Seringapatam, as a faithful mediator between Tippoo and the Commissioners. The knowledge and integrity of this irreproachable missionary *have retrieved the character of Europeans from imputations of general depravity.*"

As illustrating the "might of character" all missionary annals will sacredly preserve the name and fame of Christian Frederick Swartz.

WILLIAM CAREY.

Among the sons of the mighty, there is no nobler name than that of William Carey; and through the years his fame will increase, as men study the philosophy of history and feel the weight of character. He wrought with the hand of a master, and his works do follow him.

Born in poverty and obscurity, at sixteen apprenticed to a shoemaker, at which trade he worked for twelve years, and with very few educational advantages, there was no prophecy in his circumstances of the wide sphere that he was to fill, and the world-wide honor that he was to receive. Over the door of his humble cobbler's shop was this sign:

"SECOND-HAND SHOES BOUGHT AND SOLD."

But from the day of his conversion the Holy Spirit set the seal of a great commission upon his soul. Out of a full heart he talked for his Lord. His cobbler's bench became a village pulpit, and soon the people began to wonder where this young man had learned so much wisdom. Yielding to the call of God, he forsook his trade, was ordained to the ministry, and accepted a small pastorate with the meager stipend of only fifteen pounds a year.

His thoughts soon turned to the needy in heathen lands. Reading Cook's "Voyages," which gave graphic descriptions of the horrid superstitions and utter degradation of heathen peoples, stirred his great soul to the depths. This gave him a new interpretation of the great commission, and broadened the horizon of his faith. He saw the duty of the Church in a new and broader light. To him, further neglect was sin, and sin unto death. He appealed to fellow-Christians, only to be rebuffed and ridiculed. In a ministers' meeting in Northampton he was rebuked for his impertinence to God and his providence. He was ordered to his seat for presuming to question the councils of

God. But nothing daunted, he persevered, organized a society for the evangelization of the heathen, and became its first missionary, sailing from England June 13, 1793.

He found a cold reception in Calcutta. The East India Company refused him the protection of the British Government, so after a time he had to move out to Serampore and work under the folds of a Danish flag.

The diligent student became a great scholar, the master of Oriental languages. He was "the Wickliffe of the East," being the first to translate the Bible into the Bengali language; and with his own hand he translated the Scriptures into Bengali, Sanskrit, Hindoo, and Marathi. He also supervised the translation into other languages, until *twenty-eight* versions were issued from his press at Serampore.

The once despised missionary, by the force of his character and his extraordinary labors, commanded great influence. He was invited into the faculty of the College of Fort William as professor of Sanskrit, and became the trusted counselor of the Governor General.

All of his salary, except a few pounds on which to subsist, was scrupulously devoted to the extension of Christ's kingdom. As evidence of the world's acknowledgment of its debt to this genius and saint of God, Bishop Thoburn, in a public address, thus referred to the great missionary pioneer: "During a residence of a dozen years in Calcutta, I met many tourists from England and America. Among them all I recall but one who wished to see the house in which Macaulay had lived; one asked to see the house in which Thackeray had been born; and two or three inquired for the residence of Warren Hastings. But literally scores upon scores have asked to be led to the grave of William Carey, and the little burying ground in the old Danish settlement of Serampore has become like a pilgrim's shrine, to which Christian men and women come from all parts of the world."

Adoniram Judson, the John the Baptist of Burmah.

Adoniram Judson was the William Carey of the American Church. He had as little encouragement in entering upon his missionary career as did the "consecrated cobbler" of England. It was a little volume by Claudius Buchanan entitled "The Star in the East," that kindled the fire in his heart which at length drove him over the seas to Burmah. On his way across the Atlantic he was captured by a French privateer and confined in prison for awhile at Bayonne. But this never for a moment chilled his ardor or suggested a change of purpose. He was offered a pastorate in Boston, and urged by his mother to accept; but it had no temptation for a heart set on the salvation of heathen nations.

He expected to labor in India, but Providence directed his steps to Burmah so clearly that he could not be mistaken. Indeed, every event in his most eventful life seemed to be a signal providence, and every step was ordered of the Lord.

With perfect reliance upon God when a depleted missionary treasury promised him scant support, and with unruffled courage in presence of every conceivable danger, that man of destiny pursued his unwearied course in laying the foundations of Christ's kingdom in a far-off heathen land. His labors were prodigious, and his works do follow him.

A memorial tablet in the Baptist Church at Malden, Mass., contains this beautiful inscription:

IN MEMORIAM.
REV. ADONIRAM JUDSON,
Born August 9, 1788.
Died April 12, 1850.
Malden his Birthplace,
The Ocean his Sepulchre;
Converted Burmans
and
The Burman Bible
His Monument.
His Record is on High.

When Adoniram Judson died there were over seven thousand Christians in Burmah, in sixty-three churches, and under the oversight of one hundred and sixty-three missionaries, native pastors, and helpers. The lessons in Judson's missionary career are, the directness of his divine call, the frequency of providential interposition, the heroism of an apostolic faith, and the marvelous fruits of consecrated toil.

HENRY MARTYN.

For unreserved and unselfish consecration to God no apostle of the early Church ranked Henry Martin, of Cornwall. When the call came to a chaplaincy in India, he immediately accepted and uttered these words, which were the secret benignity and the serene contentment of his short career: "I see no business in life but the work of Christ, neither do I desire any employment to all eternity but his service." On arrival at Madras *en route* to Calcutta, after a tedious voyage, and much of it devoted to the sick and dying among passengers and crew, he wrote: "O, if I live, let me have come hither to some purpose."

Arrived at Calcutta, he soon overtaxed his frail body in order to keep pace with his consuming zeal. The hours of the day were all too short for him to master the Hindoostanee language, and otherwise be equipped for direct evangelistic work. The wretched condition of the people almost crushed his sympathetic heart. He says: "I lay in tears, interceding for the unfortunate natives of this country, thinking within myself that the most despicable *sudra* of India was of as much value in the sight of God as the King of Great Britain." In the largeness and tenderness of his noble heart he sought to rescue a Hindoo widow from sacrificing herself on a funeral pyre beside her husband. The scene sickened him, and he said that he "shivered, standing, as it were, in the neighborhood of hell."

The breadth of his brotherhood and the ardor of his sympathy expressed itself in these words: "Let me never fancy I have zeal till my heart overflows with love to every man living."

He had a discussion with a Brahman over an idol worship, in which he made this comment: "I learned that the power of gentleness is irresistible."

After spending a day in hard labor, distributing tracts, preaching the gospel, and writing on a translation of the Scriptures, the heavy-laden heart penned these words: "I was much burdened with the consciousness of blood-guiltiness; and though I cannot doubt of my pardon by the blood of Christ, how dreadful the reflection that any should perish that might have been saved by my exertions!"

He translated the Book of Common Prayer into Hindoostanee, and wrote a commentary on the parables in that language. His labors were prodigious; his liberality only limited by his resources. He supported five schools out of his own pocket.

This entry appears in his diary: "I have read and corrected the manuscript copies of my Hindoostanee Testament so often that my eyes ache. The heat is terrible—often at 98°—the nights insupportable." That version, written with the heart's blood of that frail young man, is still doing God's work in India.

He spent some time at Dinapore, and afterwards in Cawnpore. His health began to rapidly fail, but he girded up strength to complete his Persian New Testament. In order to its perfect accuracy, he went to Persia. There he completed also a translation of the book of Psalms. *En route* to Europe, overland through the country, he died— died rejoicing in Christ his Lord. His biographer says truly: "The *symmetry* of his statue in Christ is as surprising as its *height*."

JAMES CALVERT.

One of the most notable figures in missionary history is James Calvert, the Wesleyan apostle to the Fijis. His character was as robust as his faith was strong. His courage was never daunted, and the conscious presence of his Lord was the inspiring experience of every eventful day among the cannibals of the Pacific. If Christ ever indicates to his Church the men he has designated for hazardous posts, it was clearly manifest in this courageous missionary to the races in the Southern seas. A man of less physical and spiritual vigor would have shrunk from the dangers and horrors that made up the thrilling experiences of each day. He foiled the plans of many a "cannibal despot," often defended the defenseless by his brave expostulations, and frequently, by almost reckless daring, rescued "poor women and children, already doomed to be strangled or clubbed to furnish the cannibal feast."

And yet so cloudless was his faith and so great his joy in God's service, that he seemed oblivious of personal peril and unconscious of the weight of his burdens. Indeed, in a review of those early missionary years, he said: "We had no *night* of toil; God was with us from the first and all along."

He saw those cannibal islands so thoroughly Christianized that when he closed his great career there was scarcely a Fijian home in which was not daily heard morning and evening worship.

James Calvert illustrates the lofty courage and perfect consecration of a pure faith.

JAMES W. LAMBUTH.

Into this list of worthies I introduce the name of James W. Lambuth, for thirty-three years a missionary in China, and six years a successful toiler in the Empire of Japan. He illustrated the possibility of entire self-abnegation and perfect consecration to one divine purpose. Though not so richly endowed as some master spirits in the mission field, and unequal to others in vast attainments, it is doubted if the canonized roll of God's great pioneers contains a saintlier character than James W. Lambuth. No dangers daunted his courage, no difficulties swerved his sanctified purpose, and no trials weakened his indomitable will. From the hour he heard the Lord's call to the mission field down in his Mississippi home, to the day his beautiful life peacefully closed in Kobé, Japan, he could repeat the words of Count Zinzendorf: "I have but one passion: it is He, only He." So transparent was his character and so translucent his simple faith, that the native Christians of Kobé said: "He is our father, and we want him for our model."

His intense "soul-loving spirit" made him a tireless worker and gave him a tongue of fire. It is doubted if in the same length of time any preacher at home or abroad ever preached so many sermons. Others have had more eloquent lips, but there was never a more earnest tone or yearning heart. And no prophet of God ever had more absolute faith in his divinely given message. He always expected immediate results. And both in China and Japan many were the trophies of his consecrated ministry.

Dying with a heart burdened for the redemption of the heathen nations, his last words were an appeal to the Lord of the harvest. He said: "I DIE AT MY POST—SEND MORE MEN."

HON. IAN KEITH-FALCONER.

Few men have ever illustrated the divine law of service more beautifully and perfectly than the Hon. Ian Keith-Falconer. His days were short, but his influence will abide through the eternities. He was of noble ancestry. Son of the Earl of Kinton, it is said that he could trace his lineage back through the stormy periods of British history, "past the standards of Bruce and Wallace," back to the year 1010, in the reign of Malcolm II., King of Scotland, when in a battle with the Danish invaders Robert Keith won by valor the title of Hereditary Great Marshal of Scotland.

This young man was born in 1856. He loved the Scriptures from a child. His old nurse tells of his going among the cottages of the peasants soon after he was seven years old, reading the Bible and trying to explain it.

He was athletic, six feet three inches tall, and fond of manly sports. As President of the London Bicycle Club, he was champion of all England.

Engaged in mission work in East End, London, and soundly converted to God, he heartily gave £2,000 thereto himself. He studied the Semitic languages, giving Arabic chief attention, and spent a winter in an obscure place in Upper Egypt, in order to get the colloquial and study the temper of the Arabic mind, and the nature of Mohammedan religion.

He located at Aden, Arabia, only twelve degrees from the equator. As many as a quarter of a million camels come into Aden every year from the interior. This gave him access to the interior. Near there he established a mission and hospital. He studied medicine himself, that by this means he might fine readier entrance into the heathen heart. Although he bore the entire expense of the mission himself, he put himself under the direction of the Foreign Missionary Agency of the Church of Scotland.

His vast linguistic attainments led to his being elected Professor of Arabic in Cambridge. As this required only a few lectures during the year, he accepted; but most of the twelve months were laboriously devoted to mission work in Arabia. In the midst of elaborate plans for the erection of additional buildings, this consecrated young nobleman fell asleep—"quietly slept out his life while those who had been watching at his bedside slumbered with him."

His last appeal to men of wealth and culture at home contained these words: "While vast continents are shrouded in almost utter darkness, and hundreds of millions suffer the horrors of heathenism or Islam, the burden of proof lies upon you to show that the circumstances in which God placed you were meant by him to keep you out of the foreign mission field."

His death was seemingly a great calamity. But God knows best. The call for a volunteer to take his place was responded to by *thirteen young men* from the graduating class of New College.

But time would fail me to tell of Robert Morrison, the pioneer of China and the first translator of the Bible into that difficult language; of Robert Moffat and David Livingstone, and their heroic labors in Africa; of Alexander Duff, who laid the foundation for a new educational policy in India; and of Bishop Hannington, the latest martyr to Africa's redemption, who said to his executioners: "Go tell Mwanga that I die for Bagarda, and that I have purchased the road to Uganda with my life." This martyrdom and dying declaration recall those beautiful words of Bishop Alexander in characterizing the death of John the Baptist: "The mutilated body, stretched upon the threshold of Christianity, only marks the *via dolorosa*, over which the whole army of martyrs have passed to their crown." The lessons of these and many other apostolic lives, of whom mention cannot be made, will be an inspiration to the Church through all the militant centuries.

A noble company! May we be worthy of such a heritage of divine achievements! Of these apostolic spirits and their successors, we may say in the fine lines of Matthew Arnold:

> "There in the hour of need
> Of your fainting, dispirited race,
> Ye like angels appear!
> Languor is not in your heart,
> Weakness is not in your word,
> Weariness is not on your brow.
> Eyes rekindling, and prayers
> Follow your steps as ye go.
> Ye fill up the gaps in our file,
> Strengthen the wavering line,
> Stablish, continue our march—
> On, to the bound of the waste—
> On to the City of God."

www.ingramcontent.com/pod-product-compliance
Lightning Source LLC
Chambersburg PA
CBHW031740230426
43669CB00007B/413